This book is dedicated with much love to my father

and the memory of my mother

Contents

FOREWORD

As we enter the twenty-first century, we are witnessing a truly unprecedented transfer of wealth in the United States. Trillions of dollars will be passed from one generation to another, providing enormous opportunities for individuals and families to give more to their families and to charity than ever before. A wide range of people will soon experience the great personal satisfaction derived from active personal philanthropy.

To help members of the Harvard community ask and answer some of the essential questions raised at this unique moment in America's financial history, Harvard's University Development Office (UDO) has asked Charles Collier to share his thoughts and insights, which are based on the years of experience he has had as our senior philanthropic adviser.

When Charlie asked me to write the foreword to this book, I was pleased to do so. As one who has experienced the positive impact of philanthropy on my own family, I hope that *Wealth in Families* will be widely distributed within the Harvard community. All too often, when we think of our personal legacies, we focus on the "how" rather than the "why" questions. Charlie's emphasis on transferring not only wealth, but also values, has touched a strong and responsive chord among those of us who have had the opportunity to work with him.

This book is built on Charlie's personal observations, yet these cannot be fully separated from the Harvard community. Because of this fact, the UDO has decided to make *Wealth in Families* available to the Harvard constituency. Indeed, most of this book is based on Charlie's work with alumni and their advisers. *Wealth in Families* does not represent an "official" Harvard view of the world, but it does reflect UDO's mission, which is to nurture "lifelong relationships between Harvard and its donors." I believe this book has the capacity to help us do just that.

In an effort to realize many of the ideas expressed in *Wealth in Families*, I have established my own private family foundation, and I'm glad I did. My six children are on the board, and we meet every Thanksgiving weekend to discuss proposals and decide on grants. The foundation helps us to think as a team while still allowing everyone to develop his or her own philosophy about wealth and philanthropy. To be sure, Harvard often benefits from our deliberations. Our giving strategy, however, is a broad one, and our overall goal is to have an impact on society through gifts with leverage.

This book also reflects Harvard's own broad interest in fostering philanthropy, a field that has grown dramatically in recent years. The University has, for example, established the Hauser Center for Nonprofit Organizations (located at the John F. Kennedy School of Government, but University-wide in its focus) with a generous gift from Rita Hauser and Gustave Hauser. At the Business School, John Whitehead has provided the resources to inaugurate the Whitehead Fund for Not-for-Profit Management, which supports the School's Initiative on Social Enterprise. These and other Harvard programs are shining the academic spotlight on the principles and practices of philanthropy in new and innovative ways.

I am very happy, then, that this work is becoming available on a much broader basis to Harvard's alumni, their families, and their advisers. I believe it will prove highly beneficial to the field of philanthropy, to Harvard, and most important, of course, to you.

Robert G. Stone, Jr.

PREFACE

My purpose in writing *Wealth in Families* is to encourage you to think deeply about the fundamental questions surrounding wealth and its effect on your family. If I am successful, you may find yourself choosing to alter the ways in which you plan and act with regard both to your wealth and to your family.

After 25 years of working with individuals and families of wealth, I have discovered that the hardest, yet most rewarding, part of the planning process is asking essential questions about what people want to pre-serve—besides financial wealth—and how they can enhance each family member's growth.

These "why" questions surrounding family wealth are the most important ones, and yet they are rarely asked. The questions about the meaning and purpose of wealth should drive the thinking of individuals and families, and the resulting estate planning decisions and outcomes. Think about values first, products second. This book explores the meaning of wealth (Chapter 2), the amount of an appropriate inheritance (Chapter 3), family communication (Chapter 4), the development of a balanced approach to money (Chapter 5), financial education (Chapter 6), and the philanthropic impulse (Chapter 7). Several chapters include interviews with leading experts in the field of family wealth management.

Together, these pages serve as a reflection on the meaning and purpose of family wealth. These essential "why" questions surrounding wealth form the subtext of each chapter. I do not delve into the specific arrangements and products associated with estate planning and charitable giving because they are simply *secondary* to the questions of meaning, legacy, and how we grow great human beings.

As I began working with couples and families, I was led to the need for a book like *Wealth in Families* that addresses the deeper issues surrounding wealth. Exploring the complex landscape of family wealth has transformed my approach to my career and personal life. I have embraced the approach described in the book, introducing my sons to the joys of charitable giving, inaugurating a program of financial education, and facilitating family meetings for three generations of Colliers.

Conducting research and doing interviews for this book have also reinforced my conviction that discovering your calling and personal fulfillment truly eclipses money in importance. It is necessary to tell oneself and one's family this basic truth in a time of historic wealth accumulation because it is all too easy to believe we are *defined* by what we own. Substantial financial wealth challenges us to reevaluate what really matters.

At Harvard University, it is clear that what really matters are the many individual gestures of care for people and programs on a human scale. Many thoughtful gifts are viewed as "investments" that can, over time, help cure disease, improve inner-city schools, affect public policy, or train the next generation of leaders who will solve our social problems, to list just a few examples. Strategic philanthropy at Harvard and elsewhere can—and does—transform innumerable lives for the better.

This book is drawn from my career of service to secondary and higher education—more than half of it at Harvard. Against this backdrop, there are two important influences. The first is Phillips Academy, Andover, because it was Andover's deep commitment to service that set me on a trajectory that included summers of community service through the Quebec Labrador Foundation, majoring in religion at Dartmouth College, and earning a degree from Harvard Divinity School. Second, the strongest influence on my life has been the quiet yet profound example of my parents. They believed and communicated that there was something worth doing beyond our family. This principle of "giving back" has had a powerful and sustained effect on who I am and how I approach my work with families.

It is deeply satisfying to help alumni and their spouses explore the family issues surrounding wealth, shape their philanthropy, and make tax-wise gift decisions. While the book has been written for people with substantial financial wealth, its principles are universal and can be applied by almost anyone. I know that charitable giving can indeed make a difference in the lives of both donor and recipient. I hope that the questions and voices that follow can make a difference in your life, the lives of your family members, and the institutions and causes you are most passionate about.

Charles W. Collier
Cambridge, Massachusetts
November 2000

ACKNOWLEDGMENTS

I am enormously grateful to a large number of friends who have inspired my passion for philanthropy. Their openness has informed the way I think about the issues surrounding money, and indeed, the true meaning and purpose of family wealth. To all of them I owe a great debt.

I wish to thank: Joanie Bronfman, Terry Christensen, Paul Comstock, Ginny Esposito, Scott Fithian, Katherine Gibson, Lee Hausner, Jay Hughes, Alan Jones, Peter Karoff, Peter Kimball, Chris Letts, Kathryn McCarthy, Ellen Perry, Robert Putnam, Nicole Raymond, Paul Schervish, Jay Steenhuysen, Howard Stevenson, Susan Stover, and Peter White.

I especially want to thank the alumni who gave so generously of their time, experience, and wisdom, a contribution that enriched this book: David B. Arnold, Jr. AB '44, MBA '47; Robert R. Barker AB '36; W. B. Barker AB '69, PhD '75; Gregory C. Carr MPP '86; Barbara and Finn M. W. Caspersen LLB '66; Jeffrey Chambers AB '76; Abram T. Collier AB '34, LLB '37; Richard B. Covey AB '50; John A. Davis DBA '82; Charles J. Egan, Jr. AB '54; Gregory J. Englund JD '74; Michael L. Fay JD '75; Christopher F. O. Gabrieli AB '81; the Rev. Peter J. Gomes BD '68; Gustave M. Hauser LLB '55; Amos B. Hostetter, Jr. MBA '61;

the Rev. F. Washington Jarvis AB '61; William L. Jaques AB '69; John F. Keane, Sr. AB '53, MBA '54; William J. Kneisel MBA '74; Andrew K. Ludwick AB '67, MBA '69; Warren McFarlan AB '59, MBA '61, DBA '65; Andrea Okamura AB '76; Carl H. Pforzheimer III AB '58 MBA '63; David Rockefeller, Jr. AB '63; Neil L. Rudenstine PhD '64; Jennifer P. Stone AB '80, MD '86; Robert G. Stone, Jr. AB '45; Richard T. Watson AB '54, JD '60; William Weil AB '89, MBA '95; John C. Whitehead MBA '47; and William D. Zabel JD '61.

I also want to single out several colleagues whose vision, encouragement, and expertise have made a significant difference to me personally and to this project: Bill Boardman, Mary McCulloch, Geoffrey Movius, Tom Reardon, Laura Smith, Andy Tiedemann, and Frank White.

Finally, I wish to thank my wife, Sally, and my sons, Whit and Ben, for their support, patience, and willingness to let me experiment with many of the ideas expressed in this book.

CHAPTER 1

FAMILY WEALTH: ASKING THE ESSENTIAL QUESTIONS

Consider these questions:

- What is *really* important to your family?

- What are the true assets of your family?

- What should you do to guide and support the life journey of each family member over time?

- How wealthy do you want your children to be?

- Do you feel you have a responsibility to society?

These are the deeper questions families ought to ask themselves today—and on a continuing basis. I am convinced that these questions should be asked and answered before estate planning is even discussed. What kind of family do you want to be? What do you want to accomplish—or help others to accomplish? What legacy do you want to leave your children and society? Deciding where to go with your financial success and why you want to meet those goals are the strategic questions that you should ask first. Determining how to get there and which legal arrangements to use are secondary tactical decisions.

Let your shared core values and clear sense of direction guide your choices. Your financial wealth is a wonderful vehicle to help you and your family members follow their passions and achieve a collective goal. In my experience, families who go through this process achieve significantly better results—financially and emotionally.

I define a successful family as one that knows who it is, what it stands for, and where it is going. Successful families manage themselves deliberately. There is much at stake for your individual family members, for your family as a whole, and for society at large. If you and your family can define "what's important" before deciding "what to do," then your children will thrive, your family will survive, and society will benefit.

The creation of staggering amounts of financial wealth in America since World War II, and especially in the last two decades, has produced vast personal opportunity, huge inheritances, stunning philanthropy— and a crisis of meaning. The wealthy are, in many cases, searching for a dimension beyond wealth. Increasingly, they are asking themselves penetrating questions about the meaning and purpose of financial wealth. How much is enough? How do I make sure my financial wealth creates independence rather than dependency? Can I use my wealth to make a difference to society?

These broader questions are important because the arena of values and principles, communication and trust, calling and education is critical to your children's pursuit of happiness and to the positive preservation of your family. The focus of financial wealth preservation, it turns out, is not really financial.

While tax reduction, estate planning, and legal structures are important, they alone cannot enhance your children's or your family's financial wealth over the long haul. Often, estate and tax planning vehicles take on a life of their own. Indeed, empirical studies of successful family businesses worldwide reveal that transferring the financial wealth to succeeding generations is often the easiest part of the preservation and succession process.

In fact, a number of wealthy families pay little estate tax. "How can that be?" you may ask. The answer is that they plan ahead, defining an appropriate financial inheritance for their children and grandchildren. They use sophisticated techniques to transfer the financial wealth early, thereby maximizing the growth of financial assets in succeeding generations. Finally, they typically leave the residual of their estates to their private family foundation or various charities. All of these techniques may be effectively employed, however, without resolving the crisis of meaning that substantial wealth so often engenders. Financial wealth is transferred, but satisfaction is not.

How, then, should you think about the deeper issues around wealth? Begin by asking your family four simple questions drawn from a business model for strategic planning taught at Harvard Business School:

1. What is your family's vision for its future?

2. How should your family members communicate with each other?

3. How should your family encourage each other's emotional and intellectual growth?

4. How should your family make decisions together?

For me, these are essential questions family members must address if they are going to come to grips with the meaning of their wealth and complete a succession process effectively.

Succession planning is not a single event symbolized by signing thoughtfully designed estate planning documents. It is an evolving, lifelong process. Preserving your financial wealth and enhancing the lives of your family members over time is a journey. To undertake effective succession planning, you should define a family vision and mission, create a structure for decision making appropriate to your family, foster open communication, and encourage the growth and development of all your family members.

"What drives all successions is a vision of the future, hammered out over time, that embraces the aspirations of both the senior and junior generations as well as those of their forebears," writes Ivan Lansberg, a family business consultant in Connecticut. In his book, *Succeeding Generations*, he says, "This vision—which I call a Shared Dream—generates the excitement and energy that every family must have to do the hard work of succession planning."

The key questions running through *Wealth in Families* are, "What's important?" and "What's the effect of a given decision on your heirs?" They should be discussed before you ask yourself, "How do we get there?" I am convinced that these questions can be of use to *any* family, regardless of their financial net worth. Let me summarize my principal themes:

The meaning you give to your financial wealth is a statement of who you are

Your approach to wealth is a statement to your family of what you stand for. You and your family do stand for something, even if it is never articulated. What core values does your family agree on—for example, achievement, knowledge, diversity, hard work, generosity, creativity, compassion, spirituality, justice, integrity, honesty, service, respect, or love?

Another key question is, what is the meaning and purpose of your family's financial wealth? Is its highest and best use to spend it, to provide a higher standard of living for family members, to enable family members to choose careers not based on economics, to fund new family businesses, to provide a comfortable retirement, to provide for family emergencies, to provide resources for philanthropy, or a combination of all these?

Some families are quite specific about their family culture as it relates to financial wealth. The Rockefellers, for example, are explicit that their financial wealth is now devoted to preservation and philanthropy. On the other hand, the Kennedys hold to Joseph P. Kennedy's charge that the main purpose of financial wealth is to enhance the family's ability to achieve in the political domain.

Financial wealth can, however, have corrosive effects. We continually hear about intergenerational conflict or sibling rivalry around money issues that often divides or destroys families. Money is a potent force for good or ill. It can either promote or impair initiative. We all know families for whom financial wealth has provided significant benefits: freedom, independence, access, flexibility, and enormous capacity for personal and public generosity. We also know of situations in which financial wealth contributes to curtailing personal achievement and retarding maturity. The side effects can be toxic, often creating dependency and a lack of competence.

Money casts a spell—and it can be for good. It is important, indeed critical, for families to think seriously about the meaning of their financial wealth, the messages they send to their children about money, and the example they set by their own uses of financial wealth. It is my experience that the meaning given to money (and the family's core values, for that matter) is rarely stated explicitly. Financial wealth should, however, be seen as an important tool to enhance the life journey of each family member. Money can be used to express your core values and expand your family members' pursuit of their life calling. A planned program that articulates your family's values and vision, while fostering open communication and lifelong learning, can strengthen and preserve your family.

There are four major kinds of family wealth: human, intellectual, social, and financial

There is more to family wealth than the financial dimension. *Human capital* refers to who individual family members are, and what they are called to do; *intellectual capital* refers to how family members learn, communicate, and make joint decisions; *social capital* denotes how family members engage with society at large; and *financial capital* stands for the property of the family.

Families that enhance human, intellectual, and social capital have a better chance at growing great human beings, and continuing as a cohesive group that enjoys meeting, working, and being together for more than one generation.

"Most families are only aware that they have one form of capital: financial capital," says James E. (Jay) Hughes, Jr., an estate planning lawyer and family governance specialist in New York, author of *Family Wealth: Keeping It in the Family*. Hughes is a proponent of the four forms of family wealth: "A family must know whether all of its forms of capital are growing. Rarely in my experience do families measure their human, intellectual, and social capital. Frequently, members do not even recognize that they own these forms of capital."

I believe that this broader definition of *family wealth* is accurate and provides a new approach to thinking about what you should actually do with your financial capital. For example, philanthropy can be a key component of a family's social capital and can provide multiple benefits to family members as well as to society. Family philanthropy is a powerful teaching tool that provides a safe environment in which your children can learn about money management and working as part of a team. Moreover, most families of wealth want to leave a legacy of *values* in addition to their financial wealth. Philanthropy can be an important vehicle for articulating core values, providing a meaningful family legacy, and giving your children (and grandchildren) a valuable experience in competence. A program of strategic philanthropy for family members enhances their human, intellectual, and social capital.

Successful families share effective practices in common

Successful families make thoughtful choices around their financial wealth and think about the effect of their decisions on the lives of their children and their spouses, and their grandchildren. Most importantly, they talk openly with their children, at age-appropriate times, about all the issues surrounding the family's wealth.

In my experience, the best practices of successful families include the following:

1. They focus on the human, intellectual, and social capital of their family.

2. They stress the priority of *each* family member's individual pursuit of happiness.

3. They work on enhancing intrafamily communication.

4. Their time frame for determining success is long-term.

5. They tell and retell the family's most important stories.

6. They create mentor-like relationships when establishing family trusts.

7. There is a collaboratively defined family vision statement (the Shared Dream).

8. They teach children and grandchildren the competencies and responsibilities that come with financial wealth.

9. They work at getting to really know each family member.

10. They give their younger family members as much responsibility as they can manage as soon as possible.

Of course, no family achieves all of these objectives, but attempting to do so is a goal to which any family can aspire and strive for over a lifetime.

––––––––––––––

When I ask parents what their deepest hopes are for their children, they often say they just want them to be happy. But how should we think about happiness? Is it simply a pleasant emotion—or something more? According to Aristotle and his student, Thomas Jefferson, the "pursuit of happiness" has to do with an internal journey to know ourselves and an external journey of selfless service to others. Indeed, the concept of a personal moral compass has been a central motif throughout the life of our civilization.

More recently, Abraham Maslow, the twentieth-century American psychologist, gave us clues to real happiness in his hierarchy of human needs and goals. Self-actualization, the final aspiration, involves the journey through which we discover what we are truly called to do and be and get about doing it. Maslow postulated an additional objective: transcendence, the ability to move beyond the "self," to see one's own fulfillment as inextricably linked to serving the needs of others.

The Rev. F. Washington Jarvis, headmaster of the Roxbury Latin School, says that true happiness in life comes from a long-term vision of our life. Jarvis writes in his book, *With Love and Prayers*, "Important, though, as a vision is [regarding career and lifestyle], it is nothing like as important as an overall vision for your whole life. We might call such a vision existential; it has to do with the discovery by you of some meaning and purpose to your whole existence. Inevitably such a vision must entail not only finding meaning in your life but meaning also in your inevitable death." He goes on to say, "If you want to be happy, you must learn to love: to pay the price of caring for others, of putting them first, of inconveniencing yourself. That is the pathway to happiness."

Enhancing your individual family members' pursuits of happiness so that they thrive over time is a worthwhile journey. Indeed, it may be the most important journey you will undertake. I suggest that you focus on each family member's discovery and fulfillment of his or her life calling by dedicating your family's human, intellectual, social, and financial capital to that higher purpose. In the end, what we really care about is much deeper than financial wealth. The desire for meaning and genuine connection will always transcend wealth. As my father wrote years ago, "To be really rich is to be rich in achievement, rich in experience, and rich in friendship."

CHAPTER 2

EXPLORING THE MEANING OF WEALTH

"No, next Tuesday is out. Friday is no good. How about never? Is never good for you?" These are the words of the busy executive pictured in a *New Yorker* cartoon, consulting his calendar as he talks on the phone at his desk. Many wealthy individuals are indeed so busy with their business and lives that they rarely take the time to think about the bigger issues surrounding their family's wealth. It's my experience, however, that a growing number of wealthy individuals are extremely interested in the deeper issues around money and its impact on their families. Busy though they are, these people are making the time to talk about their concerns.

Paul G. Schervish, professor of sociology and director of the Social Research Institute at Boston College, agrees. He has spent part of his academic life interviewing wealthy individuals to understand their biographical narratives. He believes that a distinctive characteristic of the wealthy is the significance of the path they often take to use their wealth to care for others, "to provoke questions about the quality of wants," and "to awaken sensibilities of gratitude." Their wealth, he suggests, has the potential to deepen their sense of themselves.

"I argue that religion or spirituality encourages philanthropy by explicitly linking givers to the concerns and needs of others," says Schervish in his essay, "Wealth and the Spiritual Secret of Money." "My analysis follows a three-step logic: (1) if *wealth* affords individuals the ability to have what they want (at least in the material realm), and (2) if *philanthropy* can be understood as the transformation of time and money from a pool of wealth into a disposable gift to others, (3) *religion*—as it takes form in what I call the spirituality of money—motivates or spurs philanthropy, in amount and type, by shaping the quality of wants or desires among the wealthy. If the wealthy generally can have what they want, it is the realm of spirituality that directs their wants into a bond of care for others."

Substantial financial wealth, whether created or inherited, has the capacity to transform the wealth holder. Many wealthy individuals rethink the meaning of their money, indeed their lives, in light of the freedom and empowerment their wealth provides them. I see it in investment bankers and inheritors in their forties, who take time off to assess what they might do next with their lives. Some return to undertake a new business venture, while others become serious philanthropists; still others decide to study music or teach high school. I have watched money managers and company presidents in their fifties and sixties make dramatic changes in their lives and devote significant time and financial resources to charitable purposes. Here are three examples:

■ **Andrew K. Ludwick.** Andy is an entrepreneur. He co-founded SynOptics Communications (which became

Bay Networks, Inc., a successful Silicon Valley computer company) and was its CEO until 1997. At that time, age 51, he faced a transition:

"I took some time off because I wasn't sure what I wanted to do. I didn't want to start or run another company since I had just done that for 48 quarters. I wanted to explore other things and welcomed this midlife opportunity.

"I settled on being an investor and board member for a number of Internet start-ups in the Valley as a way to contribute to the field I know something about. I am also pursuing other interests: more personal time with my wife and children, new involvements in the local community, and a serious focus on philanthropy. Harvard was a catalyst and started me on the philanthropic track. My initial gift of networking equipment from SynOptics had a profound impact on Harvard and taught me that I could make a difference through giving.

"There was a fork in the road, and I redefined how I would spend my time and energy in many dimensions. Money gave me a set of choices, free time, and the wherewithal to build enterprises in a field that will change the world."

■ **Christopher F. O. Gabrieli.** While on leave from medical school in the 1980s, Chris founded a health-care software company that was backed by Bessemer Ventures, a Boston venture capital company. He never returned to medical school. "I was persuaded by Bill Burgin to join the firm and concentrate on health-care investing full time," he says, explaining his first career as a venture capitalist. "I liked the partners and was excited to support new ideas that turn into useful companies."

Chris took six months off in 1998 to run for the U.S. Congress in the Democratic primary in Massachusetts. Although he eventually lost, the experience proved to be a turning point and launched him into a second career:

"What began as a deep interest in public policy was becoming a bigger part of my life. I have a new career and am now involved in a number of Boston civic organizations—for example, MassINC, a leading think tank on pragmatic policy and economic planning, and the Boston Plan for Excellence, whose mission is to help reorganize Boston public schools.

"Reflecting on my past, I also realize the degree to which the generosity and foresight of others allowed me to succeed in life. I am clearly fortunate with my financial success and feel a responsibility to further the great institutions in Boston and help create new ones. For example, I think I bring something to the two committees I serve on at the Harvard School of Public Health because of my background in health care investing and policy. It's interesting, fun, and intellectually stimulating to help them meet and solve real social problems.

"My resources allowed me to dig into a second career in public policy and retool myself to acquire the skills and knowledge to make a new contribution. I had the chance at 38, rather than 58, to start another career. My money gave me the freedom to pursue my passion for public policy and philanthropy."

■ **William J. Kneisel.** After many years as an investment banker at Morgan Stanley in New York, Bill took a six-month sabbatical in 1996 to reassess his objectives:

"After years of public offerings and mergers, I discovered

it wasn't as rewarding any more. The values had changed, and there was more focus on money and transactions for their own sake rather than the earlier goals of solving client problems. The client focus that I learned from my mentors in the business, Fred Whittemore and Tom Saunders, was a kind of 'sacred trust.' I had come to the point in my life where I was calling into question what I was doing. The sabbatical gave me the time and space to reflect on where I was going.

"I thought of teaching at a business school, briefly tried working for a smaller firm, and eventually retired. I am going in a different direction now, spending more time with my family, rereading the classics, undertaking a few projects for Morgan Stanley, and enjoying lots of volunteer and charitable work for schools I care about, such as the Hopkins School and Middlebury College. My new life is still evolving, but my financial wherewithal has clearly allowed me to reorder my priorities and think through questions of meaning."

What we see unfolding is the archetype of the hero's journey: the "call," the departure, and the return. In the lives of the wealthy, it is an existential shift, often more of an inner journey than outward accomplishment. They are navigating a response to a change in their lives, frequently driven by the presence of new wealth. Consciously, they take a leave of absence to explore their options, and in this transitional work they go through a stage of development in regard to their wealth.

"Our research," says Schervish, in his introduction to the book *Gospels of Wealth*, "reveals that for many respondents—both those who earned and those who inherited their wealth—a major transformation in consciousness takes place at some point with regard to that wealth. This point may arrive quietly and gradually or appear as a dramatic realization."

Schervish uses the concept of "liminality" to explain the personal evolution of wealth holders. "Liminality denotes the boundaries between and passage through different stages of life and identity that occur at important turning points, such as becoming an entrepreneur or receiving the first installment of a substantial inheritance. By focusing on these periods of liminality, respondents highlight the intricate process of change by which they move from one stage of their relation to money to the next and hence from one stage of their identity to another."

In his book, *Succeeding Generations*, Ivan Lansberg echoes the concept of liminality with his exploration of the role of a Shared Dream in the lives of families with financial fortunes or private businesses. He makes the case that a Shared Dream, or vision of the future, is critical to the effective succession of families and family businesses. He draws on the work of Daniel Levinson, the late Yale professor of psychology, who wrote *The Seasons of a Man's Life*, to stress how the Dream can give meaning to one's life and is tied to various stages of life in developmental psychology.

"Levinson believed that the Dream is reworked during certain key transitional periods in the life cycle," Lansberg writes. "This is part of an intermittent process that combines periods of stability, in which the key elements do not change, with transitional periods, in which certain aspects of the Dream may be altered to bring them more in line with reality and the individual's internal needs."

One of the most common results of these individual transformations around family wealth is a new or renewed commitment to philanthropy. Paul Schervish heard about this phenomenon repeatedly during his interviews:

> The wealthy move beyond pursuing private interest as their public contribution to pursuing public needs as their personal concern. Those who do so may be described as having learned the *spiritual secret* of

money. The scope of their self-interest increasingly broadens and deepens to include a greater diversity of people and needs.

Financial wealth is a tool to achieve greater ends, for individuals and for society. Thus, philanthropy has a dual purpose. First, it is a vehicle for expressing core values—for individuals and for families. Typically, these values might include educational opportunity, advancement of knowledge, social justice, artistic freedom, alleviation of suffering, eradication of disease, or environmental preservation.

Second, philanthropy is the tangible expression of care for others outside one's immediate family. Schervish defines philanthropy as the social relation of care in which individuals expand the horizons of their self-interest to include meeting the needs of others. "It is the virtue of *care*," writes Schervish in an introductory essay for his book, *Care and Community in Modern Society*:

> The term *care* derives, of course, from the Latin *caritas*. The philanthropist is first and foremost a caregiver, not a giver of time and money. Time and money are the medium by which care is expressed. But the fundamental moral standard to which philanthropists should dedicate themselves is caring for others in need.
>
> Caring individuals come to view themselves and others in a different light. To exhibit a caring orientation toward others in a constant and dedicated fashion is to assume a self-definition in which one does not so much become selfless as self-expansive. A caring person is one who becomes profoundly self-concerned about what happens to others by identifying with their fate.

To explore the deeper meaning and purpose of family wealth, I interviewed Paul Schervish in his Chestnut Hill office in the fall of 1999. What follows is an edited version of an extensive interview.

COLLIER: In your experience, what do people consider to be the "meaning" of wealth?

SCHERVISH: The meaning of wealth is fundamentally freedom. It's freedom from material constraints and the constraints of time. It's a dialectic between freedom from and freedom to. The freedom to, on the material side, is to be able to purchase what you want, to go where you want, to have what you want in the material realm.

Freedom in the temporal realm is often a way of retrieving the past. When things go wrong and you have wealth, you can often correct a mistake or a problem. You can shape to some extent the present and the future.

Emotionally, wealth is freedom too. There's a psychological empowerment, a mixture of confidence that you can have what you want and you have the ability to carry it out. On a psychological level, it enables you to have both great expectations, and the confidence to achieve them.

You may remember that at the very beginning of Charles Dickens's *David Copperfield*, David says he does not know "whether I shall turn out to be the hero of my own life." Most wealth holders wonder the same thing in their contemplative moments. But for the most part, they can eventually, at least in the material realm, answer that yes, they are the heroes of their own lives. And they not only shape their own lives but also the lives of others.

COLLIER: Don't wealthy individuals often struggle with the "meaning" question at some point?

SCHERVISH: Yes, they do. But for me, this question brings up the larger issue of the effect of wealth on spirituality.

The question is this: Does wealth enable you to be more or less spiritual? Doesn't financial wealth undercut your spirituality? Or perhaps we should ask: Is the terrain of virtue and vice different for different groups of income and wealth?

These questions are becoming more important because a larger and larger number of people have more and more wealth, which not only makes the question individual but cultural. It forces one to ask, "If you can have what you want in the material realm, what is it that you want in the spiritual realm?"

I think the terrain of spirituality—of virtue and vice—is different for wealth holders. The dialectics of care and control are different. But remember, wealth is like fire. It can enchant and deepen some, but it can burn and destroy others.

COLLIER: *You have discussed the concept of "liminality" in your writing. Can you explain that term?*

SCHERVISH: What I mean by liminality is those special periods that are identifiable as psychological turning points in our lives, where we reach a crossroads or a threshold. When we leave one part of our life and enter another, it speaks of a personal transformation; a kind of life, death, and rebirth. At such times what happens in terms of financial wealth is a death of an old way of thinking, feeling, and acting around the money and a rebirth of a new way.

COLLIER: *Can you give an example?*

SCHERVISH: Yes, I talked the other day with a man who said, "Now that I am wealthy, having liquidated my business, I'm going to take a trip to Europe to consider what I am going to do next."

COLLIER: *Is this a form of the ancient myth of the hero's journey?*

SCHERVISH: Yes, it's an awakening, a vision quest. A lot of these things are happening simultaneously. It's a search for his identity. It's a search for what he's going to do with his time. It's a search for what he's going to do with his money. Not that this is a terrible fate, but on some emotional level he felt something old was passing and something new was in the offing. And he didn't quite know what it was.

Such an experience often occurs when wealth holders sell a business or receive a financial windfall, when their children grow up and move away, or when they retire. What happens in every point of liminality is that there's a transition. It doesn't mean the person becomes more or less virtuous. All it means is that they are struggling with the change of the terrain of their spiritual life. They hope that the next stage will be deeper.

When an individual has $20 million, for example, there's a liminality in which the children are seen as being part of the transformation. He may say, "I am now at the end of my time as an accumulator of wealth, and in this new period I am passing this on to my children." There is an initiation rite that goes on for the children as well as for the wealth holder. Passing the baton is a period of liminality.

COLLIER: *Many parents struggle with the question of passing on a financial inheritance. What kind of legacy do they want to leave their children with respect to their values?*

SCHERVISH: There's a spiritual legacy and there's a material legacy. Legacy is exactly what is being looked at during these points of liminality. "Where have I come from? Who am I now? How do I want to shape my future? What do I want for my children?"

Legacy and liminality are really quite intertwined. They can be handled explicitly, or [they can be] ignored and happen by default. Whether you like it or not, you're going to go through liminality. You're going to leave a legacy whether you plan to or not. If we are wise, we recognize the periods of liminality, ritualize them, and celebrate them.

COLLIER: *You've spoken of passing financial wealth to children and to charity. How do you decide on the right balance?*

SCHERVISH: That's a good question, and it already has the answer in it. The question is, How do you do the archaeology around the connection of your financial wealth to your identity and your legacy to your family? Consideration of death is the classic occasion for the exploration of the meaning of life. We hope that the prospect of death turns out to be a positive motivator to go through explicitly and productively the liminal period, asking questions like, "What do I stand for? Do I have a responsibility beyond my family?"

I believe an answer is to create significance in the light of our death, and one powerful way this is accomplished is through personal and family philanthropy. Philanthropy is financial care, but charitable giving is not the only outcome. It's financial care in many different ways. Some people transfer their business to their workers or give bonuses to the people who made them wealthy. That is as much financial care as contributing money to an inner-city school.

A lot of entrepreneurs will say that the most important way in which they're caring in the material realm is to build a business, to create jobs, and to make other people independent. The variable in all of this is not how much you give via philanthropy but how much *care* you are giving.

COLLIER: *You have said the philanthropy of the wealthy creates their moral identity, linking their destiny with the destiny of others. Can you explain?*

SCHERVISH: I believe what motivates care is identification. In the identification model the giver identifies with the recipient. Where am I most deeply developed, experienced, and expressed in regard to others? In formulating the great Aristotelian and Judeo-Christian traditions, Thomas Aquinas insisted that the issue isn't the lack of self. It's the unity of love of self, love of God, and love of neighbor. What we're seeing is the way in which wealth holders care for others as if those were often themselves—or their children.

Why is it that wealth holders give so much to educational institutions, especially those with which they are associated? Similarly, why is it that the religious organizations and churches receive so much of the giving in America? It's because this kind of charitable giving is based on their identification with others. To the extent we are looking at hungry children, or people in need of education, at a deeper level we are looking at ourselves. Identification generates generosity.

COLLIER: How important is it for wealth holders to transfer to their children a legacy of care for others?

SCHERVISH: They are going to transfer legacies of meaning as well as financial wealth, whether they think about it or not. What people ought to do is to reflect on the activity so as to do it in a better way. There are people who can't or won't do this. My parents communicated a legacy of financial care as well as religious meaning to me without going into it explicitly.

Today, wealth holders with such large estates are beginning to plan their wills explicitly, think about their estates explicitly, and strategize about how to give their money away intelligently. They are now paying attention to the way in which they want their kids to think about a financial inheritance.

The questions around financial wealth are increasingly put on the table. The question is not so much whether it's going to be done well or done poorly but whether it is to be done all at once or gradually. I think financial education is done best over time.

Nothing is irretrievable. People will say, "Well, I messed this up from the time my kids were small." Well, all that does is leave an opportunity to work anew on a deeply meaningful legacy.

COLLIER: *Is there a role for family philanthropy?*

SCHERVISH: Yes, I think you want to pass on a legacy of financial care. In some instances, it may mean a very formal and structured approach with a family foundation and a mission statement.

In other cases, you may want a strategy that allows your children to decide for themselves what to do with the inheritance, saying, "You could use this money for your own personal consumption, or you could give some of it away to improve society."

If your children make the decisions themselves, you may have given them a far better legacy. Children who make that decision have an important experience: the same decision that you once had to make yourself.

This gets to a deeper question. Does money corrupt, or [does it] open opportunity? We know the answer. It can do both. The very dynamic that we go through ourselves, wanting to make our own decisions, can provide a meaningful legacy.

We should instill a learning process by which children are always trying to figure out for themselves, with their own children and spouses, what it is that produces happiness.

COLLIER: How do the wealthy help their children to make good decisions around financial wealth?

SCHERVISH: First of all, recognize that grown children are going to make their own decisions anyway. The real question is: How do wealth holders help create the circumstances for their children to make wise decisions? For example, around the family philanthropic process, you might say, "What are your passions and how do you want to support them?" You have to allow them to give to the causes they care about and in ways and amounts that they decide.

Dealing with personal property, you might say, "I hope that this summer home or that heirloom stays in our family forever." Approach it as a desire. What you want to do is to help your children learn the process of discernment.

Education regarding discernment means that parents are guides. What you're doing is helping your children make decisions about the way in which their identity and their money are going to carry out *care* in the world.

We want to teach them how to discern what needs to be done. Caring is helping others in their true needs. True needs for others are going to change over time. What we have to do is teach people a process of caring, through wise choices, in which they connect their material means with their spiritual intention. Again, we see that empowerment and material effectiveness are linked to meaning and happiness. It's in making this connection between the financial wealth and the meaning that we find our deeper identity.

COLLIER: What do you mean by "identity"?

SCHERVISH: Their moral identity or deepest sense of themselves. I believe in encouraging an attitude where money is seen as an instrument to their true happiness.

For any child and any adult there is no perfect use of money. But there will surely be a very inadequate use of money unless the opportunity for mistakes and choices concerning money is encouraged. You might end up with your children carrying out a kind of "bronze" legacy of money— they do it your way. But if we want them to carry out a "golden" legacy with money, they're going to have to learn to discern for themselves the difference between superficial and deeper happiness.

COLLIER: *How do parents "let go" and allow their children to make choices concerning inherited financial wealth?*

SCHERVISH: Letting go of control is very difficult for many parents and more difficult for them to do with their money than, for example, with a decision about what college their children will attend.

I believe that wealthy parents have to think deeply about what really matters to them and about what their financial wealth means to them. If they think in these terms and express their thoughts, their children will listen to them.

"Letting go" doesn't mean that you simply leave your children as sheep without a shepherd. Your shepherding is your communication to them of the happiness that you create and experience by the wise use of your money.

CHAPTER 3

DEFINING A FINANCIAL INHERITANCE: HOW MUCH IS ENOUGH?

"Part of the reason for believing that my wealth should be given back to society," says Bill Gates, in a recent *Forbes* magazine article, "and not, in any substantial percentage, be passed on to my children, is that I don't think it would be good for them. They really need to get out and work and contribute to society. I think that's an important element of a fulfilling life."

Gates has touched on the defining questions: How do we provide financial security for our children while ensuring that they achieve on their own? How do you make sure a financial inheritance will help and not hinder their life journeys?

The hardest estate planning question is how much money to give to your children. The question is not how much they *could* receive but rather how much they *should* receive. How much is right for your children, and can you quantify the amount? We want our children to benefit by our family's financial wealth, but at the same time we want them to pursue a fulfilling life. How much, then, is enough? Is more always better? What is the financial wealth meant to accomplish? What is the message to our children if the primary motivation of our estate plan is the avoidance of taxes?

"How much to pass on to your children is the basic philosophical question," says William D. Zabel, a senior partner in the New York law firm of Schulte Roth & Zabel and author of *The Rich Die Richer and You Can Too*. "How much do you want them to have is a better question than how much can we get to them. Passing on all the money sends a message that financial wealth is all-important. Answering this question also leads to how, when, and in what form."

I have talked to many thoughtful alumni and some of this country's most capable estate planning lawyers on this subject, and a variety of themes—and amounts—have emerged. The issues around financial inheritance fall into four categories: how much do you give your children; when; in what form; and how much do you tell them?

How much is an appropriate financial inheritance?

What would be best for your children? What do you hope they will accomplish with the money? Making a considered and deliberate decision is wise because if you don't, *you've actually made a decision.* You have picked the default position; that is, all to my children, less 55 percent to the government. Spending time on inheritance planning may allow you to transfer the amount you eventually have in mind to your children while making gifts to charity, rather than to the government through taxes. The choices are not your children or taxes, but your children and charity and *no* taxes.

You might identify how the financial inheritance is to be used by your heirs—for example, grandchildren's education, down payment on a primary residence, maintenance fund for the family summer house, medical emergency fund, business opportunity fund, or financial security fund. Assign a dollar amount to the items and funds that you value and total the amount. That could be the starting point for thinking seriously about the financial inheritance that would be best for your children or grandchildren.

There is one other purpose of a financial inheritance that is often mentioned: the career development fund. In discussing his views on the uses of a financial inheritance, Robert G. Stone, Jr., chairman emeritus of the Kirby Corporation in New York and Senior Fellow of Harvard College, says it well: "I believe in giving your children enough money so they can follow whatever pursuit they want in life. If they want to be teachers or artists, I hope they will be the best they can be in those fields. Having money gives them freedom of choice with security, no matter what direction they decide to take."

This is a compelling approach—that is, thinking about the purpose of the financial inheritance as a tool to enhance many aspects of our children's lives. "I want to have a positive impact on their lives when it matters," says Richard T. Watson, senior partner in the Cleveland law firm of Spieth, Bell, McCurdy & Newell. "I want them to make wise choices around schooling, houses, and travel. I want to broaden their horizons, prepare them to manage the money, and help them enjoy a richer life.

"I think about the proper amount of an initial inheritance in terms of a base level of income ($50,000 to $100,000, for example) that will free them to pursue whatever career they decide is best for them. My goal is to enhance their quality of life. For me, getting them $1 million to $2 million in their late twenties or early thirties, ideally in a generation-skipping trust with the children as co-trustees, is an attractive plan."

If deciding on a financial inheritance were always that simple! In reality, thorny questions inevitably arise. Here are a few examples: "Since we are a blended family, how do I factor in my wife's children? How do I solve the issue of my younger second wife, where my children may not receive an inheritance until after *she* dies? I have been giving my older grandchildren $20,000 a year for many years. How do I make up the difference with the arrival of my newest granddaughter? Should I base my decision on the amount of the capital or the amount of income the capital will generate? My children have different needs; how do I treat everyone fairly?"

The question of fair versus equal is a difficult one. An alumnus in Boston, wrestling with his own situation, puts it this way: "How do I treat my children equally when they are not equal? They have different vocations, money styles, earning powers, and marital situations." Of course, there is no one answer because families and children do and will differ. I suggest you deal with the question directly and talk about it openly, often with your adult children. In my experience, many people will help out children during their lifetime based on need, but large inter vivos transfers and bequests of significance will tend to be equal. "You have to be flexible," adds Bill Zabel, "to take into account the differences among your children and how they change over time."

The decision on how much to give or leave your children is a deeply personal one, and there are many variables, including individual preferences and specific family situations. Having said that, and admitting there are no rules of thumb, let's make some observations using hard numbers.

In my experience, with families where the publicly traded financial wealth is in the range of $15 million to $30 million, the opening number is typically $1 million to $2 million per child. In most cases, the amount provides a measure of flexibility, but it may not dramatically change the child's lifestyle. Also, I see many people deciding that $3 million to $5 million is an appropriate financial inheritance. Finally, for families with approximately $100 million and above, many believe that $10 million to $15 million per child is sufficient. Rarely do I hear parents decide to give or leave more, except in some families with really substantial inherited wealth.

In many long-term wealthy families, there often exists a network of trusts and foundations, and an expectation that the financial wealth will be passed along to succeeding generations. "These families have a culture that inculcates the sense that you are fortunate," says Michael L. Fay, senior partner of the Boston law firm of Hale and Dorr and vice president of The Family Firm Institute. "The money has been handed to you under certain conditions. Your obligation is to be stewards and manage your affairs to maximize the wealth and pass on the principal to the next generation."

On the other hand, entrepreneurs and other self-made wealth creators often have a different inheritance strategy for their children. Sometimes, they want to pass on as much financial wealth as possible so that their children will not have to struggle as they did or to preserve a majority position in a family business. More often, however, the key concern for entrepreneurs is how to keep their children "hungry."

"Entrepreneurs enjoy the hunt," adds Fay, "and they want to instill that sense of struggle and achievement in their children. They'll set up a safety net for them so they can be teachers or musicians—to expand their range of fulfilling life opportunities. They'll tell their own story about how excited they are in creating something in the hope that their children will challenge themselves."

"How much is enough?" is a difficult question, but it is important to define and quantify an appropriate amount for each of your children. Looked at another way, the question is: How do I prevent my children from becoming dependent "trust funders"? Of course, this is a question requiring education, not a financial decision.

On the other hand, "How much is enough?" can lead us to ask the following: If financial wealth provides freedom, what does it mean to be free? "At the deepest level, the question is one of freedom," says Jay Hughes. "I believe you need to think seriously about what this means to your family.

"True economic freedom is the ability to wake up in the morning and be able to decide what you will do for the day," Jay concludes. "Thus, an appropriate inheritance may be that amount of financial wealth that will allow you to live in this way. Any amount of money beyond that is discretionary because it is not what you need to be free. More money than you need can also lead to a shadow side to freedom— which on the one hand is dependence and on the other is license, or freedom without self-discipline. This is the paradox of the question of 'How much is enough?'"

When should you transfer a financial inheritance to your heirs?

To decide on the best time to make a transfer to another generation, you must first decide on the amount of assets you will need to maintain your lifestyle for your lifetime.

If you have more than you will need, then you may be in a position to advance all or some of the financial inheritance you have in mind to your heirs during your lifetime.

Lifetime transfers, even if they are subject to gift taxes, are less expensive than testamentary gifts to your heirs. Although the estate and gift tax rates are the same, the gift tax is effectively 35.5 percent—much less than the top estate tax rate of 55 percent. The reason is that the gift tax paid is not itself subject to gift taxes, that is, it is "tax exclusive." However, any estate tax paid is itself subject to taxes, or "tax inclusive." For example, it takes only $1.55 million to give your children $1 million during your lifetime, while $2.2 million would be required to leave them $1 million through your estate.

"It makes more sense to give money to your children during your lifetime than at your death," says Dick Watson. "Leaving money to your children at your death is not nearly as tax effective. Also, the money often arrives too late to have a positive impact on your children's lives."

Moreover, early transfers of wealth to your children and grandchildren allow the money to appreciate in the younger generation—the one with the longest time horizon. Jay Hughes suggests that the model of the "investor allocator" is a way to make sure families direct new investments with high growth potential to the proper generation. "The 'investor allocator' chooses the family member or members to actually make the investment based on their proximity to the payment of estate taxes," says Hughes. "Normally, the oldest family member will buy the investment offering the lowest growth, and the youngest family member will buy the investment offering the highest growth."

So when would it be best for your heirs to receive their inheritance? In my experience, people tend to choose one of two approaches. First, define the inheritance and give it to them sooner rather than later. Talk with them, provide age-appropriate financial education, and help them understand and work with the money. Financial training and discussion of wealth responsibility are critical to this approach. Openness and access early on, coupled with education, also enhance their ability to choose careers not solely based on the economics of the profession.

Alternatively, many individuals and advisers suggest that they want to make sure their children have the chance to "make it on their own," and thus they prefer to transfer the inheritance around age 35 or later. Moreover, I know a number of people who do not want to burden their children with the issues surrounding money management in their twenties, when they should be focused on starting a career.

For many families of wealth, the answer to the question of when to transfer the inheritance lies somewhere in the middle—that is, introducing the money (and the appropriate financial education) over time. For example, give your children their college money to manage themselves. At 21, give them enough capital so they can learn the basics of investing first-hand. Add more capital at 25, and still greater portions of the financial inheritance at 30 and 35.

All of this, of course, is subject to the maturity of your children and the confidence you have in their judgment at various stages. If you have an investment whiz who is trading securities online at 17, you may want to transfer more financial wealth earlier. On the other hand, a child who is struggling to find a "calling" in his or her late twenties may be better served by receiving a partial inheritance at age 35.

"Reasonable people can certainly differ on the question of what is the appropriate age to advance the financial inheritance," adds Dick Watson. "I believe that 18 is simply too young, and giving children $100,000 at 21 may be better. A large inheritance—$1 million and up—should come later. Remember, we want the money to have a positive impact and free them to make choices in their lives. Failure to get the bulk of the inheritance to them by age 40 is just as wrong as giving them a lot of money at 18."

Sometimes you just cannot be precise. I have seen situations where the company of an alumnus is about to be sold and he transfers a large block of stock to his eight-year-old son's trust. Within months, the trust is worth $7 million, perhaps more than the parents had anticipated. Frequently, venture capitalists include their children's trusts in their venture capital transactions, often resulting in a huge run-up in the financial inheritance. Often, they ask, "I may have done the right thing from an estate planning point of view, but did I do the right thing by them?"

What form should the financial inheritance take?

To trust or not to trust? That appears to be a key question. Properly structured, trusts can have a variety of positive benefits, including long-term tax savings, while providing "control without ownership." Of course, there are other sophisticated discounting and valuation strategies that save transfer taxes such as family limited partnerships, charitable lead trusts, and defective grantor trusts, to name a few. But we should also be concerned with how the financial inheritance will be held and perceived by the inheritor. What will be the *messages* surrounding the trust? What will be the education that comes with the trust?

"Trusts make a lot of sense when you consider the issues of creditors, divorce, taxes, and premature death," says Michael Fay. "I typically make the trusts discretionary (providing a mechanism for disbursements based on trustee discretion) to ensure that the children are fully formed, achieving adults. I also want the adult children to be cotrustees (one of three, for example) and have the power to change the individual or corporate trustees."

Moreover, the quality of the human relationship between the beneficiary and trustee may be more important than the legal arrangement, says Jay Hughes in his article, "The Trustee as Mentor." "The solution to a successful beneficiary/trustee relationship lies in the trustee offering and the beneficiary accepting the proposition that at the inception of the trust, the trustee's role is to be the beneficiary's mentor and to remain in that role until the beneficiary is fully participating in the beneficiary/trustee relationship, at which time the trustee's role will evolve to the trustee as a representative."

Trusts can be a useful substitute for a prenuptial agreement when you want to preserve family financial wealth. "It's far better to create a trust that will protect your children's money from a disaffected spouse," says Dick Watson, "than to require their marriage to start off with an adversarial financial discussion, often precipitated by the raising of a prenuptial agreement."

Trusts make sense, and terms can be designed to provide great flexibility for a beneficiary. It is also clear that for most families, part of the financial inheritance should not be in trust but should go outright, with no strings attached. The lives of adult children can be enhanced with access to money for cars, houses, and further schooling. Most importantly, adult children need to have the money unfettered to *learn* how to deal with it, own it, and manage it. They need the freedom to take risks, to make mistakes, and, often, to fail. One approach is to give them a modest amount of money outright at age 21 or 25, monitor their progress, and then give them the balance of the financial inheritance around 35 to 40, often in trust. In summary, I believe that where substantial money is involved, the form of the financial inheritance should be a combination of outright gifts and *very* flexible trusts.

How much do you tell them?

People are often too secretive about family wealth. The problem with the "we're not going to talk about it" mentality is that it breeds mistrust and misinformation. Often, a lot of time and energy are spent by family members trying to find out the family secrets!

Secrecy surrounding the family's financial situation often begins between spouses. Many wealth holders don't tell their spouses how much money they have or how it is invested. An open and frank discussion is essential if spouses are going to work together on inheritance planning and eventually talk with their children. Sharing financial information with your spouse makes sense because this is the person with whom you are going to discuss sharing the information with your children.

There is also the issue of financial inequality between spouses. For example, a husband creates significant wealth and his wife has nothing of her own. Does it matter? "People don't think about the question of whether a spouse without money ought to have his or her own money so they don't have to *ask* for it," says Dick Watson. "I ask wealth holders—typically husbands—if their spouse has money of their own, and the response is often, 'No, but she can have whatever she wants.' I suggest he give his wife a significant amount of money so that she doesn't have to ask. This is often a transforming experience, changing the power and trust in the relationship for the better."

More communication is almost always better. Talking to your children *early* about the meaning and purpose of your family wealth can also enhance your relationship with your children.

"Many clients don't talk to their children about their wealth," says Gregory J. Englund, a Boston attorney and author of *Beyond Death and*

Taxes: A Guide to Total Wealth Control. "They're fatalistic about it and don't realize that the estate tax is a voluntary tax.

"Since the basic goal of the estate plan is often to benefit the children, why not include them in the discussion?" asks Englund. "Talk with your children about the family money—over time, in an incremental way. Ideally, I suggest you tell them together even if it's early for one child and late for another, for example, when they are ages 21 and 25. In my experience, this approach reduces the possibility of sibling friction around the information. Offer them some choice. They may say that they prefer to have part of their share of an inheritance go to grandchildren and to a family foundation. Share your vision with them.

"Turn around the government's default plan," Englund adds, "and you decide, in consultation with your children, how to organize your family's financial wealth. A wonderful part of this whole approach is that your children talk to one another. The expression of this concept will vary from family to family, but what a powerful dialogue. What an opportunity for your family!"

"We talked at length with our children about our money, beginning early in their teenage years," says Robert R. Barker, an investment professional in New York. "For many years we gave each of them the maximum allowable tax-free gift— $20,000 a year—and told them that our hope was that they would accumulate this for future use. Along with their grandfather, we also gave each of them $350,000 in a generation-skipping trust. We discussed everything, including asking them, 'How much do *you* think is enough?'

"I am now leaving the bulk of my estate to charity," adds Barker. "I am fortunate that I can talk to my children about our wealth and show how the rest of my money can be productive for society."

CHAPTER 4
FAMILY PARENTING: MANAGING FAMILY

The most important "assets" of your family are its individual members. A governance structure designed to enhance everyone's personal growth and development may preserve your family over the long term. Are your children thriving in their chosen calling? How do they interact within your family and with society at large? Your family will survive and thrive if each family member is pursuing his or her potential for growth and happiness.

That is the main thesis of an important book, *Family Wealth: Keeping It in the Family*, by James E. Hughes, Jr. "What each family member is called to do is the critical component in keeping the family wealthy," says Hughes. "Each human being is called to an individual life journey, and to discover one's calling is the single most important duty of each human being. A family's duty is to work to preserve the family's principal wealth-generating assets: its human and intellectual capital. The family leadership and governance structure should provide an environment that values and enhances each family member's ability to pursue their individual life calling."

As we discussed in Chapter 1, Hughes suggests that four kinds of wealth need to be preserved within families:

Human capital refers to the individual family members: their knowledge, talents, experiences, personal and shared values, skills and judgment, and their earning potential. Most importantly, the term also refers to their defining who they are called to be and what they are called to do.

"Education and training are the most important investments in human capital," writes Gary S. Becker, professor of economics and sociology at the University of Chicago and a winner of the Nobel Prize in Economics, in his book *Human Capital*. "These investments improve skills, knowledge . . . and thereby raise . . . psychic incomes."

Intellectual capital involves how individuals learn over a lifetime and how families communicate, resolve conflict, make joint decisions, and mentor each other. Families need a formal system of representative governance based on articulated family goals and values to successfully ensure that the family and its members thrive over time.

"Governance can become an anguishing issue," writes Paul Ylvisaker, former Dean of the Harvard Graduate School of Education and adviser to the Council on Foundations, in *Conscience and Community*, a collection of his essays. "In the first generation, the question is how to overcome the tendency to bow obsequiously to the founding donor; in subsequent generations, how to include a spreading avalanche of family members without being exclusive or overwhelmed."

Social capital refers to an individual's connections with his or her communities. It is a term that has been widely studied in academic circles and has been promoted as "civic engagement" by Robert D. Putnam, Peter and Isabel Malkin Professor of Public Policy at the John F. Kennedy School of Government at Harvard. "Social capital means the features of social life—networks, norms and trust—that enable participants to act together more effectively to pursue shared objectives," writes Putnam. How does your family interact with our civil society? What are your family members' inclinations for 'civic engagement'? Does your family as a whole (and its individual members) care about others beyond your family?

Financial capital reflects the more traditional definition of wealth, such as the property of the family, its financial assets, trusts, and partnerships, and other investment and estate planning arrangements.

What practical steps can you take to begin designing an effective governance system for your family?

First, hold an initial meeting of your "family assembly" to begin the articulation and documentation of a family "vision" statement. Work in small groups to ask the following questions: What are our family assets? What differentiates our family? Where does our family want to be in 20 years? What shared values do we stand for? Recruit a committee to write a family mission statement and short family history.

"Families throughout the world have created a sense of shared vision and values through the development of a family mission statement," writes Stephen R. Covey in *The 7 Habits of Highly Effective Families*. "The family mission statement is a combined and unified expression of all family members of what your family is about—what it is that you really want to do and be—and the principles you choose to govern your family life." Here is Covey's family mission statement:

> The mission of our family is to create a nurturing place of faith, order, truth, love, happiness, and relaxation, and to provide opportunity for each individual to become responsibly independent, and effectively interdependent, in order to serve worthy purposes in society.

Second, decide how you will organize yourselves to make decisions. What kind of representative governance structure do you want for your family? How often will you meet as a whole or via small committees made up of family members? What will be on the agendas?

Third, how are you going to educate yourself, your children, and grandchildren over time? I believe the key issues include the following: What does it mean to be an "owner" of financial wealth? What constitutes an effective trustee-beneficiary relationship when family trusts are used to preserve financial wealth? How can children and grandchildren best learn to make competent decisions around financial wealth, family philanthropy, and their legal and investment affairs? How can you help your children discover a calling?

I believe that most productive individuals who contribute to society find a personal calling. For inheritors, this does not mean that they must work for wages, although the family culture may dictate that it is preferable. Work of any kind is important to self-esteem. A recent *New York Times* story on the death of one Harvard graduate captured this point: "And yet his money and his background, or the effect they had on people, conspired to set him apart. He never really found a calling."

"Financial capital alone cannot provide long-term wealth preservation," says Jay Hughes. "What a family's financial capital can provide is a powerful tool to promote the growth of its human and intellectual capital. After all, without human capital there are no family assets; there is no family! Without intellectual capital, undereducated family members with all the money in the world will not make enough good decisions over a long period of time to outnumber their bad decisions. Successful long-term wealth preservation lies in understanding that it is the growth of a family's human and intellectual capital that determines its success, and that the growth of its financial capital provides a powerful tool to achieve this success."

To expand my understanding of Jay Hughes's philosophy, I interviewed him in Chicago in September 1999:

> COLLIER: *Explain the phrase "shirtsleeves to shirtsleeves in three generations?"*

> HUGHES: In every culture that I've encountered—in China, Latin America, and Europe, for example—I run into the same proverb. In China, rice paddy to rice paddy; in Ireland, clogs to clogs.

> It appears that financial wealth is destined to disappear in three or four generations. The proverb means that the first generation makes the money, the second generation preserves it, the third generation spends it, and the fourth generation must re-create it.

> I prefer the rice paddy idiom; for example, imagine a poor couple in China wearing torn clothing. They pull rice every day and make a financial fortune. They don't leave their home or change their way of life.

> The second generation moves to the city, joins the opera board, and becomes significant members of society. The third generation, having no experience of work, spends the money, and the fourth generation goes back to working in the rice paddy.

> COLLIER: *Why does the third or fourth generation tend to dissipate the family financial wealth?*

HUGHES: Basically, they do not learn to work. Work in its deepest dimension equates to a calling. Discovering your calling is the most important task an individual can undertake, and to do this successfully requires that you seek a mentor and become an apprentice to learn what you are called to do and be in life.

Successful families ask the fundamental questions. Who are you? What is your passion? How can I enhance your life journey and your pursuit of happiness? These are the most powerful questions a parent, friend, or mentor can ask. In fact, each generation must in turn re-ask these critical questions around passion and calling.

I believe that the mission of the family is to enhance the individual pursuit of happiness of each family member. Successful individuals keep the entire family growing and thriving. That is the heart of my philosophy, and what I see successful families practicing.

COLLIER: *What do you mean by "family governance"?*

HUGHES: I am talking about the process of joint decision making. I am convinced that a family, like any endeavor, must develop a way to make decisions, resolve conflicts, and find some level of consensus.

In families that have moved from the sibling generation to the first-cousin generation, you find for the first time large numbers of individuals who didn't grow up in the same household. Thus, you need a structure for those first cousins to be able to form the consensus necessary to make decisions. If you move to second cousins and great-grandchildren, you're now looking at a very diverse set of upbringings. Again, if you then don't have a formal structure for getting together and making decisions, it's very unlikely that they will have much in common—except the family's financial wealth.

If a family wants to survive for a long time, I think it is critical that it evolve a governance structure appropriate to itself to afford an opportunity to make those decisions that need to be made jointly.

COLLIER: *What would be an effective governance structure?*

HUGHES: Human beings almost always end up in governance structures with three branches. First, they set up a *family assembly*, which is the policy-making branch to which all members of the family are welcome. In my opinion, the spouses should be included.

Many families then involve the members of the family assembly in committees to carry out the wishes of the family assembly during the period between meetings. Often, one of these committees becomes a form of family executive and is frequently referred to as the *family council*.

The most advanced families create a third branch, the *judicial branch*, establishing a council of elders who resolve disputes, help the family define its vision and mission, remind the assembly when it's not following its rules, and assure that the family stories are told. (Only elders, who have wisdom and know the family stories, can perform that function.)

COLLIER: *What's the role of a family mission statement?*

HUGHES: First, let me make a distinction between vision and mission. A shared vision is critical to a family. It is the leap of faith that a family can take together that says, "We are a family, we share a vision of what the family is, and we wish to stay together to perpetuate that vision."

Mission is the carrying out of that vision. It's the expression of the process of the vision. I think that's an important distinction.

Having said that, I believe strongly that if you don't know where you're going, you won't be able to get there. The mission statement for a family is its statement of the direction in which it wishes to go and what kind of family it wants to be. What is frequently missed by families that disappear is that they fail to articulate and share a common vision and the mission that carries it on.

What is critically important is that the mission statement flow downward to all the entities in which the family does things together—for example, in their philanthropic work, their investments, or operation of a family business.

COLLIER: *How does a family apply your lessons?*

HUGHES: Have a family meeting, and ask a number of critical questions. First, each member should be asked, "What are you passionate about, and who are you to your friends?" Get right to the question of passion. Go to the question of journey.

Second, ask this question: "What's this family going to look like in 20 years?" Work together on what you want your family to do and to stand for in the future.

Talk about forms of family governance. Are you a democracy? Are you a dictatorship? How do you make decisions and resolve conflict? How would you like to make decisions?

The fourth element is learning that with privilege comes responsibility. You have to get used to the responsibilities of the different roles in families, whether it's as a trustee, beneficiary, shareholder, or grantmaker. Each of those roles requires responsibility to obtain the benefits of privilege.

Again, you start with a family meeting and work through those four elements. That way you will create a family that functions well as an enterprise.

COLLIER: *Do you think a family should hold one meeting a year?*

HUGHES: I think one general meeting a year is absolutely obligatory. By the way, a lot of time at the meeting should be given to telling the family stories. They are the glue. It is through these stories that we learn best who we are as a family.

Do you need to have two or three meetings a year? Maybe. It depends on the work that has to be done. If your family has a number of enterprises, businesses, family trusts, or philanthropic funds, then the family council, for example, may need to meet with the assembly more often than once a year to discuss what needs to be done.

COLLIER: *How do children learn to deal with financial wealth?*

HUGHES: One of the insights I've gleaned over the years is the fundamental mismatch in people's minds between management and ownership. Every child born into a family of privilege automatically becomes an *owner*. Each becomes a stakeholder in the family as an enterprise, an owner of the heritage of that family and of a portion of the financial wealth.

Every single person in such a family should be taught how to be a great owner, knowing that very few are going to be called to financial careers. Since I believe that financial capital is simply a tool to enhance the growth of the human, intellectual, and social wealth of a family, it follows that human, intellectual, and social wealth can grow only if all the family members understand their roles as owners of the enterprise. They are free to pursue their own calling, but they must accept responsibility as owners of the enterprise that is a family.

Stewardship, to me, is another way of talking about ownership. Many families, in trying to deal with this issue, confuse ownership/stewardship with management. Management is a science. Ownership, on the other hand, is the art of conserving and stewarding.

COLLIER: *What is the role of philanthropy within the governance structure of a family?*

HUGHES: I frequently use philanthropy as a learning tool for the operation of various family enterprises. After all, a family philanthropy has to learn to invest because it has an endowment, which must be managed prudently. It has administrative, management, and grant-making components. Therefore, it is a training ground for the basic administrative and management issues that are found in all enterprises.

Most importantly, you have to make joint decisions around the foundation's grants. You have to learn how to create consensus, access requests, listen carefully to the other points of view, and make sound judgments. You learn how to work together. These same lessons apply in all endeavors within the family.

On a deeper level, philanthropy is a way for your family to express its values—for example, the principles of giving back and improving society. Family philanthropy is at the core of what I mean by social wealth, giving to the outside world of your time, talent, and treasure.

CHAPTER 5

PSYCHOLOGICAL PARENTING: MANAGING ONESELF

"Is the financial success of parents detrimental to the development of emotionally healthy, productive children?" asks Dr. Lee Hausner, a Los Angeles–based clinical psychologist and author, in her book, *Children of Paradise: Successful Parenting for Prosperous Families.* "Does high parental achievement put children at risk? Do the hard-won advantages that well-to-do parents are rightfully proud to provide their children automatically create problems that outweigh the benefits? What happens to the basics of good parenting when we add the advantages and disadvantages of wealth and power that come with affluence?"

Most parents would agree that they hope their children will develop into "emotionally stable, competent individuals who can make a contribution to the world, " to use Hausner's words. However, the presence of substantial wealth—whether inherited money or the explosive wealth from venture capital—can make parenting even more of a challenge. Do you raise children differently in the context of substantial financial wealth?

"While effective parenting is an arduous task for all mothers and fathers, and some parenting pitfalls are universal, affluent parents and their offspring face a unique set of problems," Hausner points out in her book. "Just as poverty has a profound influence, so too does affluence. It creates distinct problems as well as opportunities.

"High-achieving parents often apply the same business skills and acumen at home while raising their children, and they fail to realize that a different set of attitudes and behaviors is necessary to ensure that their children develop into adults with productive and fulfilling lives. An effective parent must be open-minded and willing to question the correctness of their own attitudes, able to admit a mistake, and receptive to new learning. Successful parenting involves a special set of skills and orientation that cannot be directly taken from boardroom behavior."

In fact, the sense of control and insistence on perfection that works well in parents' business lives is often not useful in the family setting. "Children need to be nurtured and encouraged," Hausner points out, "and they need tolerance when they make mistakes, as well as the willingness to allow them to make their own choices. Above all, they need opportunities to take charge of themselves and to assume personal responsibility if they are eventually to manage their own lives."

Time is a precious commodity in our lives. Many well-meaning parents unintentionally limit their availability to be with their children because of important business, social, and charitable commitments. "While it is not possible to create universal rules regarding time," Hausner says, "learning effective parenting techniques can make the time you spend with your children meaningful, memorable, and special, so that you are, in a sense, *with* them even when you are not." Many observers have pointed out that the quality of time we spend with our children is just as important as the quantity.

Another challenge in raising children in the context of wealth is how to give them a balanced sense of the role of money in their lives, ensuring that they make the connection between work and reward—that is, the value of money. "If affluent parents do not actively instill within their children a sense of value and respect for money and the effort earning it requires," asserts Hausner in *Children of Paradise*, "the result can be a child who not only believes there is an endless supply of capital but one who consequently abuses it."

Further challenges include being realistic in your expectations of children, helping them to develop their own competencies and thus avoiding unhealthy dependence on the powerful adults surrounding them. You should learn to be an excellent listener, communicating in a manner that demonstrates respect for each child. Finally, take responsibility for a financial parenting program.

People are not born with well-developed parenting skills. Therefore, Dr. Hausner suggests that parents commit to a process of learning how to enhance their parenting skills. Participating in a communication workshop or enrolling in a parenting program such as the "Systematic Training for Effective Parenting" (STEP) are excellent beginning steps. Additionally, there are many useful parenting guides such as *Children: The Challenge* by Rudolf Dreikurs.

The family is a fluid, continually evolving, emotional system. Each set of relationships (parent to parent, sibling to sibling, parent to child) affects the entire family. In the often-changing world of the affluent family, such issues as financial difficulties, stress-related illness, divorce, and frequent job changes and relocations can all have a significant effect on the interactions within the family system. Parents need to examine their daily actions in terms of the impact they have on the larger context of the family.

To gain a better perspective on these issues, I talked to Katherine Gibson of Charlottesville, Virginia, who heads a consulting firm, The Inheritance Project, Inc., which focuses on the emotional aspects of wealth. She told me about three challenges she and other inheritors have commonly experienced:

> When I was younger, I felt a subtle form of isolation, and this was especially acute after college, when I was working on my own and saw the financial limitations firsthand that most people live with. I had an uneasy sense that I was somehow "different," just because of my money.

> Another experience that I, and many inheritors, have had is guilt—the feeling that you have this money simply because you were born into it. My sense of guilt is now gone, however, because I've actively made good use of the money for my family and for society.

> For some inheritors, the sense of guilt is exacerbated by how the family wealth was acquired, for example, through a tobacco company. Fortunately, that was not the case in my family. My parents' messages around our family business and wealth were positive, and there was always a sense that our family business had a responsibility to its community.

> A third issue is one of empowerment around money. For many inheritors, the money is there for their benefit, but it's *not* actually theirs since it is often held in trust. It requires a kind of double mindedness to come to terms with money that is both yours and not

yours. The question becomes "How do you form a relationship with money when it's ultimately controlled by someone else?"

All of these issues have an impact on one's self-esteem. I've worked and feel competent, but I've never had to struggle financially the way other people have to throughout their lives. I am very conscious of these emotional issues and think deliberately how best to raise my two children in regard to our family money.

Dr. Lee Hausner and I met in Florida in March 2000 to talk about the most important psychological issues surrounding wealth.

COLLIER: *What are the key issues connected with the psychology of money?*

HAUSNER: Few people feel comfortable talking about money. It's the last conversational taboo. We discuss everything else, but issues dealing with money cause a variety of negative feelings and so little is usually said. Even the phrase, "If you have to ask how much it costs, you can't afford it" reveals the idea that money is not something that we should discuss. Yet money is vital to life and should not be denied. It's something that we need to learn to manage and to deal with strategically. Teaching these skills to the next generation is part of one's parenting responsibility.

Money by itself is no longer just a commodity for barter. It has become a substitute for things such as power, control, love, happiness, and self-esteem. It is basic to our lives, and individuals must learn how to control money and not let it control them. We live in a world of money. Unfortunately, there is insufficient information available regarding its effects on our children or how to use it wisely.

COLLIER: *How do you raise productive children who are responsible with wealth?*

HAUSNER: I feel that the critical goals for successful child rearing are twofold: to raise a child who is emotionally well integrated and to raise one who has developed sufficient competency to make a positive contribution to society.

If these are the goals, then the question to be asked is, "In what way does money enhance or detract from the ability to create such a child?" Obviously, money enables parents to provide all the basic needs, including wonderful educational and travel opportunities. But the downside is that money can also negate the need for achievement.

If you already have money without the necessity of working, it becomes easy not to develop the discipline and focus that lead to competency. Children who are raised in an impoverished environment are forced to become independent and competent because there is nobody providing for them. Whatever they desire must come through their own effort.

What happens to a wealthy child surrounded by people who do things for them: tutors, nannies, and strong parents—a whole world of people whose main function is to service this child? When does this child have an opportunity to become competent?

The critical issue is the lack of work experience. If you read autobiographies of great achievers, most of them struggled and had significant work experience. They sold newspapers, they worked on the docks, they worked in a store. They *really* worked hard, and this type of work is one of the important competency experiences.

Contrast this to the world of wealthy children. If they're not in school, they're often in summer camp or traveling in Europe. Not only do they often miss the opportunity of working, but in families of generational wealth they don't even see the model of work in their families. The source of the family's financial support is a trust fund. In these situations, how are they going to get the idea about what it means to work?

Work is important because it is a method of validating oneself. Additionally, it gives the individual the opportunity to experience the "high" of achievement. When a child becomes addicted to the excitement of achievement, then money will not impair their productivity.

I have had the opportunity of working for the past two years with a number of the new technology millionaires. Many of them come from middle-class backgrounds, and their primary concern is that their newfound riches not destroy the middle-class values that they feel are so important. And when they speak of "middle-class values," they refer to the importance of work and being productive. Because the world of investing, philanthropy, and financially indulging their children is new to them, they are open to learning the skills necessary to effectively handle all aspects of their new wealth.

COLLIER: How do parents provide financial security, yet create opportunities for meaningful work that leads to self-actualization?

HAUSNER: Parents have to give their children opportunities to be competent as often as possible. This means that from the time your children are able to do anything for themselves, they do it. In spite of the fact that your family might employ full-time help, children need to be assigned specific chores for which they are responsible. These might include setting the table, cleaning their rooms, and feeding pets. Additionally, I think you must stimulate them intellectually. Talk to your children and ask for their opinions.

COLLIER: Entrepreneurial parents have said to me, "I have a seven-year-old child, and we're flying in our private jet to Jackson Hole. I'm worried about the message I'm sending my child. How do I raise children with a balanced view of our family wealth?"

HAUSNER: This is a big challenge. What the parents might say is, "We happen to be extremely fortunate, and we have this jet that we can use on special occasions. Most people are not able to use this airplane, and we do not talk about it because it will make people feel unhappy or jealous. This is a luxury item that is available because your mom or your dad worked very hard."

COLLIER: What if the financial wealth is inherited?

HAUSNER: Then the "script" changes somewhat. What you say is, "We are very lucky because Grandfather or Grandmother worked very hard to create the wealth we enjoy. But very few other people are going to be able to have the advantage of this kind of resource. It means that we need to get ourselves as competent as possible so that we can manage our money well because if these resources are not managed, we could lose what we have."

COLLIER: What steps can parents take to help their children realize their social responsibility?

HAUSNER: I think it is critical for families of wealth to expose their children on an active basis to people who are less fortunate so that they have the opportunity to appreciate how fortunate they really are. For example, go to a homeless shelter and spend a morning a month—not just giving money—working with the kids, so that your children get a chance to see how lucky they are.

COLLIER: What can parents do to minimize the "entitlement syndrome"?

HAUSNER: The issue of entitlement is a real concern. It is the issue that Robert Coles discussed in his book, *Privileged Ones: The Well-Off and Rich in America*. He was the first one who really talked about entitlement and how that sense that some children develop that the world *owes* them can, in fact, cripple them emotionally. (His book came out just about the time I went to work for the Beverly Hills school system.) Parents have got to set limits and tell their children they're not going to get everything they want— even if the family can afford it.

COLLIER: *When do you think children should receive their financial inheritance?*

HAUSNER: I feel strongly that parents should not give their children a significant financial inheritance during their career-building years, say, ages 22 to 35. I don't mean that you shouldn't help them out financially with their needs around health, education, reasonable housing, philanthropy, entrepreneurial activity, and financial education. But in terms of when they are going to receive a large inheritance, it shouldn't be during those important career-building years. I don't think they should get it until they're around 40. They need to make it on their own if they're going to achieve any kind of competence. Money can derail the work they need to do during career-building years.

Building a career is not easy. There are tasks and challenges that most young adults would want to avoid if they could. And often the motivation to stay focused and disciplined in these situations is the actual need to support oneself. Excessive funds make it easy to walk away. But the result of the hard work and effort is the eventual "high" these young adults receive when they achieve on their own. At the end of the day, when your child looks in the mirror and says, "This was a life well led," it will be because they felt they were an achieving individual.

Any time we derail that sense of accomplishment, there is cause for concern, and too much money too soon is a potential for derailment. If career building extends to 40, then I believe they need to make it on their own. The difference with the young "dot-comers" is that they did it themselves. It wasn't given to them. And even if the money "goes to their heads," at least they have earned that right. They know they can achieve.

COLLIER: You don't think parents should fund their children's lifestyles until they're much older?

HAUSNER: Not until they have a chance to make it on their own and have the joy of saying, "I followed my passion and can manage my own life." I am also in favor of supporting children following a passion that is not financially rewarding—like social work or teaching. Parents could, for example, match the earned income so that children making this career choice would not be financially penalized. Making the world a better place could be an important value in your family, and you want to reward that kind of passion.

COLLIER: Should all the children know that Mom and Dad are going to subsidize the social worker in the family?

HAUSNER: Yes. I am a firm believer in family meetings from the time your children are very young. Regular family meetings provide a natural forum for talking about issues like this. In this case, you might have a family discussion about matching earned income up to a certain amount so that all family members would be aware of their options.

Of course, you wouldn't have to match the income of a child who is a successful investment banker, but it is important to talk about it before your children even make those choices. I think you have to talk to your children about these issues before they go to college and start thinking about careers. You might say, "One of the uses of our money is to help you meet a minimal level of economic life. If you want to be a social worker or an artist and you make a career choice based on your passion, which is not financially remunerative such as teaching, social work, or the creative arts, this is what your family will do to support that choice." But it ought to be a match to the amount that your child earns independently.

COLLIER: *Should wealthy parents continue to work?*

HAUSNER: I have been asked that question by young entrepreneurs who now have more money than they will spend in their lifetime and want to leave their current job. My response is that if at least one parent isn't working, their children will not see a model of work in their family and may not understand the value in working and being motivated to work themselves. If wealthy parents want a more balanced lifestyle, they can model the "work ethic" of discipline and focus through philanthropic endeavors, a second career, or pursuing an avocation in a professional manner.

COLLIER: *Is it possible that financial wealth can derail relationships within the family?*

HAUSNER: When money is used as a substitute for parental love, "things" will become very important. If one family member perceives that another is receiving more "things," envy and resentment will derail relationships. However, if a child has a strong sense of self-worth and a genuine feeling of connectedness within the family, then the financial wealth will not disrupt the family.

COLLIER: *What is the role for mentors in families?*

HAUSNER: I think mentors play a vital role. The more positive relationships you can expose your children to—which is really what the mentoring relationship is—the more this child is going to grow and develop. Mentors are often very important in families, because sometimes it is hard for parents to be mentors. Often they're so close they can't separate and they get too involved in the achievement of a child. As a result, they can't be as objective as a mentor can be. The opportunity to be mentored by an aunt, an uncle, or another family member becomes important.

Mentors can be outsiders too. They can help children in business, philanthropy, and career development, for example. Or suppose you have a friend who's just a very wise individual. You may ask that person to mentor your child. What you're doing with a mentor is finding characteristics that you would like your child to be exposed to.

Aunts, uncles, and grandparents have, for years, served as mentors. Very often a child will say, "The most significant influence in my life was my grandfather, who had the time to talk with me and taught me important things about life." These are wonderful mentoring relationships.

COLLIER: *What do you think about prenuptial agreements?*

HAUSNER: I believe in a prenuptial agreement because healthy relationships should not be based on finances. A prenuptial agreement is a business contract, and with the high rate of divorce that occurs, families should protect the business or financial assets of the family. It protects wealth that was created before the marriage. Signing a prenuptial clearly indicates that money is not the motivation for this marriage.

I think the problem with prenuptials is that the parties involved are not able to discuss it in a comfortable way. Often, the concept of a prenuptial has never been discussed until someone comes home engaged. Obviously, there will be apprehension when this proposition is presented to the other party.

Families of wealth should talk about prenuptials from the time of their children's adolescence. They need to explain the importance of the wealth protection philosophy of the family and how this will enable the financial wealth to grow for future generations as well as providing lifetime benefits to the current generation. Family money should have nothing to do with the love between two individuals who wish to marry. When discussing this idea with future in-laws, it is important to emphasize that even with a prenuptial, everyone will benefit from this type of financial wealth preservation. There can be trips, vacation homes, educational trusts for children, and retirement security, for example. The prenuptial doesn't take any of that away. Additionally, the new couple will have the full benefits of the wealth that they create together, and this should be seen as a priority.

COLLIER: *What about family philanthropy?*

HAUSNER: Philanthropy is an important part of the social capital of a family. Parents should be clear in transmitting the message that when a family is fortunate enough to have significant wealth, there is an obligation to give back to society and that part of the financial wealth transfer planning of this family will involve charitable giving. This is an important message to give children and helps them to include the needs of others.

COLLIER: *What is the role for philanthropy in helping children to become competent?*

HAUSNER: One of the benefits of philanthropy is that it involves collective problem solving around grant-making activity and gives family members an active experience of how to be cooperative and collaborative.

I think they also have a chance to become educated financially. You can talk more easily about assets that don't belong to the family but are going to be used to improve society. I think the great thing about philanthropy is that children are often exposed to other mentors, people who are philanthropic.

COLLIER: *Finally, why is it important to think about the psychological issues around family wealth? What is really at stake for families and for the individual members?*

HAUSNER: There is a lot at stake because you don't want to leave the development of your children to chance. You need to be strategic, develop a plan, and tell your children explicitly what they can expect in the future.

The message in my family was, "I expect you to take care of yourself, to earn your own way, and to support yourself when you're out of college." That was a very clear message. My two children never thought they were going to come home and live indefinitely. They just never even considered any other option because that was the message that we gave them.

We also gave them the best education they could have, and we said they could stay in graduate school as long as they wanted. That was the rule. As long as they're in school, they get funded. The minute they are not in school, they don't get funded. This is their life, and I'm not going to foster lengthy dependency. It's time for independence. Graduation day is independence day. I believe you provide them with all the tools they need to achieve. That is one joy of having money: you can give your children all the tools that they need to be competent and independent adults.

CHAPTER 6

FINANCIAL PARENTING: MANAGING MONEY

"We did some financial education indirectly over time with our children when they were young," says John F. Keane, Sr., chairman and CEO of Boston-based Keane, Inc., a leading IT software consulting company. "More recently, we talked about financial education directly when we set up trusts for our three children and gave them some money outright. The money is at risk, but their ability to use their judgment and experiment with it is part of their learning curve. I believe it's a good idea to think and talk about financial education for your family."

Today, it is easy to conclude that financial education for your family is a must. After all, financial education is a form of your family's human capital that needs to be enhanced over a lifetime. There is too much at stake to leave the "basic training" about money to chance and hope that your children will absorb pertinent information by osmosis.

Kathryn M. McCarthy, director of client advisory services at Rockefeller & Company in New York, says financial education is critical. "It facilitates the preservation of the family's financial wealth," says McCarthy, explaining why you should take educating the next generation seriously. "Today, we are inundated with financial information and advice—good and bad—and we all need to be conversant in the basics of wealth management in order to interpret the information and to ask good questions. This is especially true for all members of wealthy families.

"It's a part of your life. You have to become financially savvy sooner because the world is more sophisticated. Money is a hot topic, and there's more information that is coming faster, especially on the Internet. Moreover, enlightened advisers are willing to bring family members—even if they are young or lack experience—into the picture. They know that all family members have a stake in decisions about money."

How do you give your children the skills to manage inherited wealth? How do you best prepare them to handle an inheritance? What should you do in the way of financial education? Raising financially responsible children isn't easy—either for children or for parents—and yet the stakes are high. If wealth holders want their children to become competent in using their financial inheritance wisely, then I believe they should implement a financial education program and tailor it to the *individual* needs of their children. There is much to learn about saving, spending, philanthropy, working with investment professionals, understanding trusts, and personal budgeting.

Here are four things you can do to get started: set an example, provide guidance, allow consequences, and use mentors.

Set a good example

Most developmental psychologists say that our parental modeling has a powerful influence on our children's behavior, even if not immediately. Some have asserted that the way parents talk with each other about money is also important. Therefore, the first step toward instilling a sense of financial responsibility regarding family wealth is your own example and the messages you send to your children by your behavior with money. How should we act? For starters, we ought to exhibit prudent spending habits, put some limits on luxuries, talk about the economic aspects of family life, and tell our children why and where we are philanthropic. These positive practices send children profound signals about money and its role in our life. Thoughtful parental modeling around spending and philanthropy will positively affect our children.

"Of course parents have to be positive role models," adds McCarthy. "First of all, they need to understand their own family history around money and how well or poorly *their* parents performed as role models. For example, I recently talked to a middle-aged woman who had never written a check. Her husband took care of the family finances, as was the case in her mother's generation. She was recently widowed and now has to deal with valuable stock options from her husband's estate. Despite a good education, she patterned herself financially like her mother. It will take an enormous effort for this woman now to be able to understand recommendations from her advisers and the consequences of that advice."

Provide consistent guidance

A deliberate plan of financial education is just as important as your example in ensuring that your children learn to handle their inheritance properly. Handling money well is a life skill that is best learned gradually over time. As children grow older, they can take on more responsibility and handle more sophisticated financial tasks and concepts.

You can begin early, for example, at age 5 to 7 with an allowance. Even something as simple as an allowance raises sharp questions. Should an allowance be a payment for chores? What are the consequences if they do not do the chores required for the allowance? What is a responsible amount?

Here is a list of age-appropriate steps you can take to educate children:

Grade school, ages 6 to 12

Discuss caring for possessions.

Structure an allowance: Most experts suggest a modest amount for being part of the family and doing certain basic household chores.

Provide jobs for pay.

Encourage long-term savings: Consider matching any money they will save for over a year.

Set limits around money, for example, not buying everything they want when you go shopping.

Introduce philanthropy: help them to give and take them on site visits.

Teen years, ages 13 to 18

Insist on summer employment; fund their Roth IRA.

Guide them through their budget and a 1040 tax return.

Advocate smart consumerism: For example, discuss the messages in advertising and the impact of advertising on their purchases.

Discuss the intelligent use of credit cards and checking accounts.

Explore investments on the Internet (see Appendix C for a list of financial Web sites).

Engage them in philanthropy: encourage site visits and include them in evaluating gift decisions.

College years, ages 18 and over

Work with them on a college spending budget.

Insist on summer employment and fund their Roth IRA.

Set up adviser-facilitated learning about investments.

Provide money for them to manage.

Explain the roles of trustee and beneficiary, if trusts are used in your family.

Engage them in philanthropy; add them to the board of your philanthropic fund.

Allow them to make mistakes

Let your children make mistakes with their own money, such as spending money on toys that go out of fashion or break immediately. It's often a mistake for *us* to bail them out when they make bad decisions. Help them understand what they still have to learn or what they might do differently. Children need to learn early and often that they are responsible for their decisions—including those that involve money—and must live with the consequences.

"I think young adults in their early twenties should have some money ($10,000 to $20,000) and be told it is theirs to do with as they please," argues McCarthy. "They should be allowed to spend it, invest in their friends' movies or Internet companies, for example, and possibly lose it. And if they make mistakes, they can learn how to deal with the consequences—both financial and personal—such as losing a friend or trusting the wrong person. Mistakes with money can be an important learning experience, but they can also provide an opportunity to discuss what went right or wrong—while avoiding blame or embarrassment."

Consider the use of mentors

Businesses have had formal mentoring programs for years and have found that this kind of executive "coaching" can be very successful. Applying the same strategy to financial education in families with wealth can also be effective.

"Studies show that caring teachers and firm, wise coaches greatly influence the course of many young lives," says John R. O'Neil, president of the Center for Leadership Renewal in California in his book, *The Paradox of Success*. "Once out of school, we largely do without the aid of teachers, but the need remains. They (mentors) can be supportive yet objective, using their outside perspective to help you see the larger pattern of your development."

As mentioned in the last chapter, mentors can be family members (aunts, uncles, grandparents, for example) or nonfamily outsiders such as teachers, advisers, or friends. The arrangement can be formal or informal. Mentors provide a rich apprenticeship experience, educating young people on financial matters, helping with personal and career aspirations, furthering their long-term learning, and supporting them when they fail. The important point is not to overlook the option of mentors as a way to provide the financial education you desire for members of your family.

"My parents' generation thought a lot about how to raise responsible children," says William Weil, chief operating officer of eAgents.com, an Internet company in New York. He explains that the older generation realized that if they wanted the younger generation to be responsible, they had to give them responsibility first:

> Responsibility took many forms, including communicating the details about the family's wealth, ongoing financial education, granting limited investment

decisions (where mistakes could be made), and learning about and participating in family philanthropy.

The education around family investments and philanthropy for me and my 16 cousins and siblings started
seriously as soon as we each reached age 18. Our parents were clear about the dual purpose of the wealth: to
enable us to live well while pursuing diverse careers
and to allow us to support causes we cared about.

Now everyone has an equal understanding of what's
happening with the investments in their trusts, while
recognizing that people are different and some are less
interested in the financial education. What's been helpful to us is the openness and communication around the
money and its management.

I asked Kathryn McCarthy to expand on the issue of how a family
can start a program of financial education for children. She is a financial
adviser in New York, trained as a lawyer and also in finance, who has
served the family offices of the Rockefellers and Sulzbergers. She con-
ducts financial education programs for individuals and families throughout the United States.

*Collier: Why should families undertake a program of
financial education for their family members?*

McCarthy: I think the first question is: Should families talk about their wealth at all? Should families develop a
philosophy about their wealth before deciding what kind of
financial education to create? Is financial education useful?

It's been my experience that if families focus on
what the money means—creating more wealth for future generations or undertaking family philanthropy, for example—
these families develop the necessary values around money
that can be articulated to current and future generations.

Developing a core set of values around the use of money contributes to the overall health of the family and sustains it through many financial decisions. If there is no discussion, then they may be denying a part of who they are as a family.

So before we ask the question, "Why financial education?" we need to ask whether families should talk about money in general and what money means to them as a prelude to financial parenting.

Collier: *Why do children in wealthy families need financial education when investment professionals are available to them?*

McCarthy: There are many reasons. First, society presumes that they know something about their money. They have to operate in a world that is fueled—rightly or wrongly—by financial considerations. It's expected of them.

But more importantly, knowing the way financial, legal, and trust matters work actually helps the family communicate. Family members can develop a common and often unique way of looking at their finances. I've experienced families who develop their own language as a way to express financial and legal concepts.

Financial education also allows a family member to maintain his or her individuality because if he or she wants to build on knowledge, they can do so. I see financial education as a way to foster family harmony and to promote family communication.

Collier: *Are you saying that some base of knowledge puts all the children on equal footing?*

McCarthy: Yes, and that's another reason why financial education is important. Families and their structures around money change. There are deaths, births, divorces, investment windfalls, and financial reverses. Ultimately, the family as a whole has to take responsibility for their money. It's understanding that with the wealth comes opportunity and responsibility. One of the responsibilities of being a wealth owner is to be educated about your money.

The kind of education that I'm referring to is basic financial knowledge, including information surrounding personal finance, investment management, and legal structures that allow you to follow a conversation about your wealth and ask questions of people who advise you with confidence.

Wealthy individuals are typically advised by a series of advisers, either outside professionals or the staff of their family office. Therefore, individual family members must have enough knowledge to assess whether the advice is relevant, timely, and appropriate. You can't do that in a vacuum; you need to develop at least the sense of what's going on in the financial world at large and in the family's financial environment. My experience is that almost everyone in a family is called on, at some time, to be a part of decisions about the family money, and they need to prepare for that.

COLLIER: *Who should provide the financial education?*

McCARTHY: In my view, the parents should initiate the process with their children at a young age. I was recently with a family psychologist who said that she never heard any complaints about people giving information too early. But she had scores of stories about the problem of giving the information too late.

The trusted adviser and, often, the family office can continue the groundwork laid by parents. I know a couple with bright young children who were interested in the stock market. The parents had their investment adviser talk to the children about stocks and bonds. The children are now investing in mutual funds and getting information online.

Many families have formal education programs that are often held around family meetings. I recommend that parents include outside advisers in the process so that the next generation becomes accustomed to the way advisers work and the different kinds of advice they give. There also should be different faces in front of a next generation, not just the *parents'* advisers.

I have a situation where I'm a trustee of a trust for the sole purpose of educating the next generation, and I am not an adviser to the senior family members. This was a conscious decision and has worked with great success.

I view financial education as a journey, and there are a number of phases. It begins when children are young, answering the "what is" questions and defining concepts like stocks, bonds, philanthropy. It moves to the teenage years, answering the "how to" questions such as how one invests or makes grants. In adulthood, the "integration" question comes up; for example, how does an investment program fit in with various family trusts? Sometimes it's not until they are 40 or 50 that they see how it all fits together.

There are also education programs sponsored by institutions like the Council on Foundations. These are devoted to educating family members. There are conferences, workshops, summer camps, and retreats on financial education. Parents want their children to be educated, and many understand that they can't do it all and that their advisers sometimes are not the appropriate people.

COLLIER: *Is there a role for grandparents?*

McCARTHY: Yes, grandparents are an excellent resource. They have financial wisdom through experience, even if they lack technical expertise. They are good teachers, having practiced on their children. I've often observed a kind of magic when grandparents teach young children financial concepts.

COLLIER: Who is this financial education for: parents, children, grandchildren?

MCCARTHY: Financial education is for everyone. We focus on the younger generation because they often need it the most. Spouses and in-laws are important too. One way to get in-laws involved is to have them be part of an educational program. They themselves can learn and transmit knowledge in a different way to the family members.

I think financial education is for the whole family. This may sound trite, but the family that learns together is going to have a way of communicating with each other and can become stronger by the common experience.

The older wealth holders—and the newer "dot-com entrepreneurs"—need to be careful not to be so busy making the money that they don't take the time to transmit some level of knowledge to their family members. If they can't learn together, they should inspire the next generation to learn on their own. Wealthy families have a wonderful opportunity to do this because they have the resources to make it happen.

COLLIER: At what age do you start financial education?

MCCARTHY: Neale Godfrey has written a useful book, *A Penny Saved*, suggesting you should start at age three. I think you can start early—at age five or so—with simple concepts like saving, spending, and giving. One can't begin a program based on age alone. The program must be tailored to the learning style and ability of the child. It's important, particularly in a larger multigenerational family, to have family members of similar ages learning together.

COLLIER: What about the teenage years and the use of the Internet?

McCarthy: We have a fabulous opportunity with teenagers because the Internet is a tool they really understand. There are hundreds of great Web sites like Motley Fool that have all kinds of information and interactive programs for teenagers. It seems that more sites are being developed daily. Teenagers especially need this resource because it enables them to learn on their own. It's empowering for them to learn at a pace tailored to their own learning style. But they're not going to get everything off the Internet, and it can be isolating. Make sure they have access to other forms of learning with their peers and from other individuals.

In some of the programs I've held for wealthy families, I approach it like teaching a class. There was a group of 16- and 17-year-olds and 18- and 19-year-olds. They worked together and reinforced each other's learning. It has to be fun, relevant, and at a level they can understand.

Collier: What kind of financial education works well with twentysomethings?

McCarthy: Working with children in college or in their twenties can be tricky because of the time constraints and distance. They're going to graduate school, starting careers, and traveling, for example, and therefore organized programs may not be the best vehicles for financial learning.

I think that individually structured programs and mentoring, in addition to regularly scheduled programs, can be the most important way to reach this age group. For example, let's take the 25-year-old woman living in Boulder whose family is in New York. Her parents' adviser could help her to design a program, which includes finding a mentor, a professor at the University of Colorado or a local lawyer, for example, along with a plan for attending night programs or lunch discussions at a brokerage firm.

There are a lot of new communication tools for families: conference calls, email, and family Web sites. Information about programs can be posted on a family Web site or through email from another family member—for example, "This is what we're thinking about doing, and we're going to have a meeting on the new family partnership or the subject of asset allocation. What kind of information do you need from me or the family office?"

COLLIER: *How can parents be realistic about financial education for their children?*

McCARTHY: You start the education early because you may lose them in their teenage years. Once children go out into the world and are subject to peer pressure, you can't expect them to adhere to a program of financial education. They can be more critical and often tend to follow their friends because they don't want to be different. But in the normal course of development, they typically come back in their twenties and see the value of the education.

COLLIER: *When do you conclude the financial education for your children?*

McCARTHY: I don't think you ever stop because the family system and its needs are always changing. In many cases, the financial status of the family may remain static for years and then change dramatically for whatever reason: births, deaths, or divorces.

If one can learn key concepts—what is inflation, what is a trust—basic information is formed like a foundation on which a house can be built. For example, a family may not need or want trusts, but if there is a disabled child, the need may arise. Having some familiarity with trusts would allow a more focused discussion on the issue of trustee selection and the use of a trust in this situation.

And remember, I'm talking about financial education in the sense of ownership of wealth and being able to ask good questions. It doesn't mean your children have to be able to trade stocks and bonds, draft a will, or know the technical components of a family limited partnership.

Collier: Does the family philanthropic fund offer a place for financial education for children?

McCarthy: Yes. It's an ideal place to begin and continue financial education because there is an investment and financial component to a family's philanthropic program. A foundation, for example, can serve as an educational tool for teaching investment concepts as well as the financial concept of budgeting.

The philanthropy program is also a great way to engage individuals in the younger generations who don't typically have any say in the overall governance of the family yet. The next generation can receive financial training and observe the way financial decisions are made and their impact by participating in the family philanthropic fund.

I'm currently involved with a family foundation where in order for the younger generation to move into a broader role in the family business, they had to demonstrate that they could successfully manage the process of giving away money. They had to know how to budget for grants, understand the foundation's investment program, and how to communicate with their advisers. It was a wonderful microcosm of what they would ultimately have to do in running their family business. I think family philanthropy can provide the beginnings of an individual's understanding of the decision-making process and how different financial disciplines integrate with each other—for example, investments and taxes, or budgeting and investments.

It's also a way for younger family members to learn to appreciate what money means. Many families are unwilling, at certain ages, to tell the complete financial picture to their children and yet are willing to discuss information about the foundation's assets and goals. In fact, the foundation is typically a source of family legacy and pride.

COLLIER: *There's a lot of information out there. How much financial information should you give your children?*

McCARTHY: The minimal amount of financial education would be the equivalent of what you would learn in a course on personal finance. Those courses include something on income taxes, the economy, investments, insurance, trusts, estate planning, and the various legal entities that are used in wealth transfer—limited partnership interests and forms of corporations, for example. You also need to know the basic tools and definitions surrounding charitable vehicles.

COLLIER: *Are there other skills that children need to learn that are related to financial education?*

McCARTHY: I can think of several. Part of financial education involves some training on the skills of how to make joint decisions and resolve conflicts. In a business sense, this means knowing how to negotiate. Negotiation is a part of business and financial life, and it's certainly an important part of communicating within families. Family members need to understand something about the art of negotiation. There are wonderful books out there—*Getting to Yes* by Roger Fisher, for example—where you are given fundamental ideas on to how to negotiate and influence decisions.

Also, many family members will have to make a presentation at some time to a charity, at their family meeting, or even to the public. Gaining the competence to deliver presentations is another useful skill. Think about the financial people that you admire; they are all fairly articulate speakers.

These are life skills, and they relate to financial education. Some family members might like to work on these skills before they tackle financial concepts, so this approach can be a way of engaging family members who are not necessarily drawn into financial subject matter.

COLLIER: What have other families done in the way of financial education?

McCARTHY: Many families have a formal education committee that deals with the family's financial education at all levels, from the seniors down to the 5-year-olds. As part of their family meeting, the education committee reports on programs that they've structured during the course of the year. In fact, part of the family meeting is typically devoted to an hour of financial education for all generations.

I know a family that set up an investment club for their teenagers and younger adult family members. The investment club has a chairman and meets quarterly. Initially, the members attended a two-day intensive program about investments. Each family member was given a research assignment and made decisions about stocks. Their results were measured, which was a hot topic of discussion within the family. Theirs was a true success story.

Education at family meetings can be useful. It's a great time to present a new concept around the family's overall estate planning, such as the creation of a family limited partnership. This gives the family as a whole a chance to learn about the new legal structure, understand terms and expected outcomes, and ask questions. There can also be follow-up information during the year as the plan is put into effect.

COLLIER: How does a family know whether it's been successful with a program of financial education?

McCarthy: The family needs to constantly reassess its program. The critical measurement is your family's ability to make decisions as a group about a common financial issue and not leave anyone out of the process because they don't know enough to participate. Being inclusive in family financial discussions is a big indicator. Each family member should have the satisfaction of being able to ask a good question of an adviser and have the answer given in an appropriate adult manner.

Another way of defining success is to look at your family philanthropy. A foundation that is run well in the eyes of the senior and junior generation of the family is an indicator. Remember that the family's philanthropic fund is the "think tank," a tool for charitable giving and financial training.

Finally, I think the most important element is to assess the education along the way. I see programs, often designed by family offices, that are not successful because the family or the family office staff didn't say, "Give me some feedback. Is this educational program working? Does it address your individual needs?"

Successful families understand that they are always learning, that there is no magic solution, and that people learn in different ways. There should be no point at which a family stops trying different things, and if they make financial education fun, interactive, and continuous, it will succeed. Ultimately, success is when the artist in the family is comfortable with a discussion of the family's financial assets—and shows up for the meeting!

CHAPTER 7

PHILANTHROPIC PARENTING: MANAGING FINANCIAL CARE

Philanthropy can instill a sense of responsibility around wealth in the next generation of your family. "The more money you have personally," says Bob Stone, "the more responsibility you have to society. Providing an inheritance to our children also gives *them* certain responsibilities as well, including using their wealth to have a positive impact on society."

Family philanthropy (organized charitable giving involving the donor and/or relatives of the donor) can be an effective parenting tool with many benefits. Including your children and grandchildren in charitable giving decisions—even with small amounts of money—can help them in developing the following skills: understanding financial concepts such as investment management, due diligence, and analytical evaluation; learning to work together, make joint decisions, and solve problems; and even public speaking. Moreover, you can pass on core values, such as generosity and volunteerism, and encourage their individuality through their own giving. Philanthropy can be a competency experience for children, and they can be introduced to the process in their early teenage years.

"Families need to think about involving their children no later than their teenage years, because otherwise you may lose them until they are around 30," says Virginia M. Esposito, founding president of the National Center for Family Philanthropy in Washington, D.C. "What can you do? Expose them to board meetings, create a junior board that recommends grants, take them on age-appropriate site visits, and encourage them to volunteer. Think of yourself as a mentor helping them to understand their own social commitment. After all, someone inspired you. Finally, tell them why you give and about the satisfaction you experience with your own charitable giving."

Philanthropy can also strengthen your family as a whole. Many families state that their family philanthropy is not only rewarding but has brought them closer together. Paul N. Ylvisaker states the benefit this way in his article, "Family Foundations: High Risk, High Reward" in the *Family Business Review*:

> The returns on a family investment in philanthropy are—or can be—extremely high, both internally and externally. When such an investment is well executed, a family can achieve the cohesion that comes with a sense of higher purpose and cooperative effort. Family members report an excitement and fulfillment going far beyond what they had known as related members of a tribe. Accepting the challenge and educational experience involved in assessing public needs and evaluating grant proposals from the point of view of the public interest is an incomparable experience and one that can build strong bonds among family members.

Virginia Esposito agrees with Paul and expands the role of the family philanthropic fund: "In my experience, family philanthropies have goals for both family and for society. If you understand that, then you can attend to both. There is often a healthy tension between the two. Your family philanthropy is not just about giving, and it's not just about family. The benefit for your family is the experience of working together on something larger than yourselves, producing a different kind of family engagement and meaning. For younger family members, it expands their horizons about what is possible in the world. The benefit to society is having private money invested in a public purpose."

"Our family foundation gets us together and keeps us connected, even if only by speakerphone!" says Jennifer P. Stone, director of oncology at Nashoba-Deaconess Hospital in Concord, Massachusetts, and daughter of Bob Stone. She continues:

> My generation is a diverse group, and we lobby for the causes we care about. I want to support education and the environment and last year directed a gift to the Quebec Labrador Foundation, an international community development and conservation organization I had worked for during college.
>
> My siblings and I are trying to assess the effectiveness of the gifts to a variety of causes—from providing access to Outward Bound to funding research on Lou Gehrig's disease. We're all on email and do some of the research on the Web.
>
> We often disagree on the best strategy to leverage our family giving. Will a large gift to a charter school be effective? How does it help society? We're also discussing ways to measure outcomes. We don't have a formal evaluation plan, but we're working on it.

To organize your family philanthropy intelligently, I suggest you explore the following four areas: defining your core values, choosing a giving vehicle, making grants, and transferring leadership.

Defining your core values

Deciding on what you want to accomplish is the first step in planning your family philanthropy. What values does your family stand for? Can these principles guide your family philanthropy? These questions suggest that a discussion of what values, principles, and virtues your family can agree on may help inform and focus your family's philanthropic priorities. To what extent does your family share a set of core values while still making room for individual preferences? (As couples, you may want to work through a short questionnaire, and I have included two sample questionnaires in Appendix A.)

Families have used a number of exercises to help determine the scope of their philanthropy. For example, you can ask each family member to list five values or principles they care about the most. Alternatively, pass out a list of values—honesty, fairness, compassion, respect, commitment, accountability, justice, generosity, spirituality, and personal achievement, for example—and see if a consensus emerges around a few core principles that might shape a focus for your family philanthropy. What kinds of organizations do we want to support or which social issues should we address that reflect our core values? Of course, a formal set of shared values or articulated focus may not be that important to you or your family, but the *conversation* you have with your family members around values and principles may be useful.

"Once you involve family, you have to ask, 'What do you stand for?'" says Esposito, explaining the value for families of articulating the purpose of their philanthropy and writing a mission statement. "Does everyone who is involved understand and share a common commitment? You should answer these questions before you begin to think of a mission statement for your family philanthropy. This is a 'statement' to your family, friends, and the public describing what your giving is about. It needn't handcuff you or restrict your reach, but it provides a shared sense of purpose. Its greatest value may be the conversation it produces within your own family."

Choosing a giving vehicle

The choice of a legal structure for your family's philanthropy should follow deliberation of what you want to accomplish and why. Esposito elaborates:

> Other good questions to ask about family philanthropy include the following: Whom do you want to involve? Why involve them and how? Once you answer why and how to involve your children and what your grant-making interests might be, then you can decide whether to have a private foundation or not, whether to have a process for giving or not.
>
> Many families choose multiple charitable vehicles. For example, they might use a private foundation, a donor advised fund, a supporting organization, or no structure at all. I've seen families that use staff, advisers, and research. I've also seen wealthy donors simply write checks.

Most wealth holders use one or more of the following legal entities: private family foundation, supporting organization, or donor advised fund. The private family foundation provides a donor and his or her family complete control over the grant making and investment management while the supporting organization allows the donor and family shared control. Family members must constitute a minority of the board of a supporting organization. The donor advised fund provides individuals and families with advisory influence without investment and administrative worries.

All of these vehicles have similar benefits. You are allowed to make income- and/or estate-tax-deductible gifts to an entity while retaining the ability to influence or control—to varying degrees—how and when the funds are distributed. For a more detailed look at these vehicles, see the descriptions in Appendix B.

Making grants

To be effective, families have a number of decisions to resolve around their grant making. Here is a preliminary list of the critical questions that you may find useful in discussing philanthropy with your family.

Goals and strategy

- What issues will be the focus of your family's philanthropy?
- Do you want to support a wide range of projects or focus on just one, or very few?
- Do you want to help solve immediate social problems, invest for long-term change, or both?

Engagement

- Do you want to be proactive or reactive to issues, that is, a capital provider or an engaged partner?
- Do you want to give independently or collaboratively with other funders?
- Do you want to support established organizations, seed new projects, or both?

Assessment of grantees

- Who will undertake your due diligence research and site visits?
- What questions will you ask to assess the organization's leadership, expertise, financial strength, and chances of success?

Grant making

- What will be the size of your grants?

- Will they be one-time or multiyear grants?

- Will you fund unrestricted support, specific projects, grass-roots innovation, or research?

Measuring outcomes

- What will be your criteria to effectively assess the success of your grants?

- How will you know if you have been successful?

- Should you commit money to measure outcomes?

"What do you want to know and why?" says Christine W. Letts, executive director of the Hauser Center for Nonprofit Organizations at Harvard University and lecturer in public policy at the John F. Kennedy School of Government, discussing the issue of evaluation. "If you want to measure outcomes, you can hire an expert to undertake science-based evaluation and get a report. But the critical question is: 'What will you do then? Will the evaluation of performance inform your decision-making process?'"

Transferring leadership

Should a family philanthropic fund continue past the donor's generation or go out of business? If it is going to be maintained long term, how do you plan the succession of leadership? This is an issue that should be explored early on in the life of your family's philanthropic fund. It is especially important for families that have made a commitment to a private foundation with substantial resources. There are compelling arguments on both sides.

On the pro side, a family philanthropic fund that lasts for multiple generations has the potential to keep your family together and transfer core values to future generations. Since many individuals who create foundations involve their children early on, they are often optimistic about the next two generations' ability to make thoughtful decisions.

A case can also be made for stewarding financial resources to solve *tomorrow's* social problems. I heard one funder say that "foundations are designed to put long-term money toward solving long-term societal problems. They balance other forms of giving that are more immediate."

The argument against perpetuity for a family foundation often rests on the question of public policy: Given the modest five percent payout requirement, are private foundations skewed to future generations? Should foundations give more today to solve pressing social needs as opposed to enhancing asset growth for tomorrow? There is also the question of the inevitable shift in donor intent. Many foundations are unable to adhere to the founding donor's intent, given changing family situations and new issues in society. Some families decide that making a significant impact now is more important than existing in perpetuity.

"If you arrange for your wealth to be available in the year 2100, rather than addressing current social needs, the funds may be dispersed in a manner that the long-forgotten donor cannot possibly anticipate by expressions of intent," asserts Gustave M. Hauser, a proponent of a "sunset provision" for foundations. "Many would be well advised to give away most of the money during their lifetimes or require that all funds must be spent within a specific time frame—for example, 25 years."

Given the variety of private family foundations in terms of size, staff, and program, the answer to this question will vary greatly.

Solutions that others have chosen to resolve the issues concerning foundation longevity include the following:

1. Keep the foundation going and trust the succeeding generations to make effective and responsible decisions.

2. Bring on a substantial number of outside trustees to professionalize the board.

3. Include a specific provision in the foundation's charter to "sunset" or dissolve the foundation (after 20 years or the grandchildren's generation, for example).

4. Allow family members or trustees to determine later whether the foundation will continue long term.

5. Fold the foundation's assets into a community foundation or into one or more nonprofit institutions, or convert it to multiple donor advised funds for individual family members.

6. Hire outside staff to have your foundation evolve into a public operating foundation.

"Succession planning for your family philanthropic fund is a serious issue," says Virginia Esposito. She adds:

> Once you get to the third generation, maintaining family cohesion is often difficult. Geographical dispersion, lack of shared values, conflicting influence of spouses, and absence of the founder all contribute to possible abandonment of family philanthropy. Like the succession planning for any enterprise, you have to plan and continually ask, "What do we want to accomplish?"
>
> You also need a structure and shared values that make it easy for everyone to stay committed: (1) Inspire them to participate, (2) train them to be able to participate, and (3) plan how they will participate when there are, for example, more than 35 cousins involved. In short,

how are you going to empower them and involve them when they all can't be on the board? Many families don't think about the issues of succession and perpetuity of their foundation until it's too late and an emergency arises—for example, when Mom or Dad dies. You have to find a way to think about the issue now.

There is something very special about the commitment of a group of people to one another when they share an equally heartfelt commitment to something greater than themselves. There is great passion and compassion.

What follows are some brief narratives from Harvard alumni who have been thoughtful and effective in managing their individual and family philanthropy.

■ **Robert R. Barker**. "I set up the JMR Barker Foundation, our private family foundation, over 30 years ago," recalls Bob Barker, general partner of the New York investment firm Barker, Lee and Co. "My primary motivation was involving our children. I wanted them to see how much fun it is to give."

Bob has been an active philanthropist throughout his life and has made generous gifts to many causes— Harvard College and the American Museum of Natural History among them. However, the focus of his family's foundation giving has been on venture philanthropy:

"We've put up money to research specific problems in Central America, for example, to help preserve the rain forest in the Amazon Basin, and to start a telecommunications program in Eritrea. We have translated the venture capital model from my business to our family philanthropy. We've taken lots of risks; some grants have not worked out, but others have produced bigger rewards. Besides the colleges, schools, and museums we care about, we have, for example, supported the following: the North Atlantic Salmon Federation; Jackson Laboratories; Americares; Life Span Systems; Prep for Prep; the Vermont Land Trust; Tibetan U.S. Resettlement; and the original planning for modernizing Grand Central Terminal.

"We don't have a staff or a specific focus. The only criterion is that one of the trustees must know the cause or institution intimately. There are ten trustees: six family members and four outsiders drawn from friends, advisers, or business associates. The balance of the trustees is always with the family, and all of my children are on the board.

"We meet twice a year to make grant decisions and discuss the investment results of the foundation. One of the benefits of our foundation is that it has been a vehicle to teach my children about investments, because the agenda of our meetings covers the foundation's portfolio. So they have learned over time.

"Regarding our succession plan, I can say that I have just resigned as chairman of the foundation and my son, Jim, has taken over. Also, my granddaughter, Margaret, a consultant at Trilogy in Austin, Texas, has just joined the board. She's very excited and has ideas and causes that she wants to support, including a project in Boston to enhance wheelchair sports. She wants to keep the foundation going.

"This foundation has been a major force for our family. It's been a wonderful focus twice a year, bringing the family together to discuss causes that are most important to us, individually and collectively. It's been a thrill for me and my children."

Bob's son, Ben Barker, former president and CEO of

Data Race, Inc., a communications products company in San Antonio, agrees that the family aspect of their foundation has been important. "The foundation has caused our family to stay in touch, whereas without it we might not see each other," says Ben. "For me, the two most valuable reasons for having a foundation are these: First, it helps the family dynamic by bringing us together; and second, it forces us to think about how to make the world a better place through the institutions we care passionately about. I don't think we would have invested the time and effort and resources without the focus of the foundation."

■ **John F. Keane, Sr.** "I started thinking seriously about the meaning of our wealth at a symposium at Harvard Business School a few years ago," says John F. Keane, Sr., in explaining why he and his wife, Marilyn, decided to create a family foundation. "We broke into small groups to discuss 'What is family?' and I came to the conclusion that what is most important is the perpetuation of core values. Eventually, we decided that one way for us to perpetuate our values was to engage our children in a process—family philanthropy—whereby we would discuss and debate how to give away money effectively."

Working with their three grown children and their children's spouses, the Keanes developed a foundation mission statement to reflect their deep interest in helping children:

THE KEANE FAMILY FOUNDATION
Mission Statement

The Keane Family Foundation is dedicated to making a difference in a world of many needs. We feel that this can best be done by encouraging role models among young people at risk. As a family foundation, we seek to further the values we hold high: respect for oneself and others, belief in individual empowerment, reverence for learning, and faith in the ability to make the world a better place. Our focus is to support programs that can inspire disadvantaged youth to improve their station in life, build their future, and contribute to the betterment of society.

In order to maximize the impact of its resources, the Foundation is limiting grants to youth in the communities in which we live. We are interested in funding organizations, new or established, that will have significant impact through programs that show promise of long-term success. These programs may involve the examination of issues or the implementation of solutions. Through its grants, the Foundation strives to champion children in crisis, nurture integrity and ambition, provide opportunities for enrichment and growth, and promote involvement and performance while building a strong sense of family and community.

This focus has prompted the Keanes to create the Keane Family Scholarship Fund at Harvard College, and in 1993 to help start a nonprofit organization called the Project for Young Negotiators. This organization in Charlestown, Massachusetts, teaches negotiation skills as a way to curb violence in the inner city. The Keanes provide seed money, ongoing support, and personal involvement in helping this organization go to scale nationally and internationally. "The joy I get is seeing the impact," says John.

"Wealth provides a base of security," adds John, discussing his philosophy of money and the issue of succession in the family foundation. "But after that, it's a tool to reaffirm, nurture, and extend the values that we care about as a family. Our wealth, on the next level, is a vehicle to reach out and to invest in others.

"We have the family members capable of administering and managing the foundation, and keeping alive the values that our family stands for. The problem is not the next two generations, but several generations down the line. I think it's just a matter of time before we, as a family, will have a series of rigorous discussions on the future of the foundation."

■ **Carl H. Pforzheimer III**. "My grandfather was a philanthropic person," says Carl H. Pforzheimer III, managing partner of Carl H. Pforzheimer and Co. in New York. Together with his parents and children, Carl has been a member of one of Harvard's most loyal and supportive families:

"My grandfather started our family foundation in 1942 and eventually left a portion of his estate, including his personal library, to it in 1956. A portion of his library was disposed of over the years by the family, bringing in a large infusion to the foundation. Charitable giving is very important, and our foundation can be useful to a society with lots of problems. I come to this belief by way of my father and mother.

"In the early 1990s, my sister and I decided it was time to get the next generation involved in the foundation. We each asked one child to join the board. Her designee has been the same since then, and two of my children rotate onto the board every two to three years. The other is in the Foreign Service and posted abroad much of the time. There are also two outside board members: a business colleague and an educator.

"Our typical minimum gift is $25,000. Our maximum multiyear commitments are generally in the range of $5 million. We meet four times a year, and I talk with the board about how, why, and what we want to give to.

"Our grant making is family-driven, not market-driven, and we operate with a strategy of tiered involvement. Our first priority is to give where foundation trustees and family members are deeply involved—typically on the boards of various nonprofits. There is recognition within the family, and the nonprofits for that matter, that our foundation giving is deliberately linked to personal involvement. Our core giving has been to Harvard, the New York Public Library, and Mount Sinai Hospital, among others.

"The next ring of foundation giving, moving out of the core circle, is 'light' family involvement, and the final tier is supporting causes and issues that we and our friends feel strongly about. We give a great deal to education and scholarship and health care. We don't generally give to 'annual giving,' but rather to specific causes such as Concert Artist Guild, Careers through Culinary Arts, the Dance Theater of Harlem, Pace University, Teach for America, the Henry Street Settlement, Horace Mann School, The Morgan Library, White Plains Hospital, and the South Street Seaport, which lie in this final tier.

"I will remain involved as long as I can. The children will continue to be involved and one of them is likely to emerge as the leader of this family enterprise. We have talked about a spend-out, but I see no reason to do so. It is my hope that the foundation continues into my grandchildren's generation and beyond. It is great fun, is good for our family, and is helpful to society."

- **Andrea Okamura**. "I love sports, and joined the Harvard tennis team as a walk-on in my junior year," says Andi Okamura of Atherton, California, explaining the genesis of the gift she and her husband, Jeff Chambers, made to Harvard. In 1999, they made a substantial commitment to the College for women's athletics. "I learned a lot about myself playing on the team—about my willingness to take risks and how I deal with winning and losing. It was a great experience for me. I am a big believer in athletics for everyone, and my gift will enhance women's participation at the College."

Besides playing tennis at Harvard, Andi sang in the Collegium Musicum, took voice lessons, and eventually completed an MFA in music performance at Boston University. Today, she is an active volunteer for a number of Bay Area institutions, including the schools that her two sons attend, Sacred Heart and St. Joseph's.

She is also on the board of the East Palo Alto Tennis and Tutorial program and runs its annual fundraising dinner.

"We teach tennis and arrange for academic tutoring for underprivileged kids in East Palo Alto. The program has been very successful in giving them a sense of accomplishment and an experience in teamwork. I've followed a number of kids in the program, and some have gone on to great things. It's part of our community, part of our lives, and I love that.

"Jeff and I give to Harvard, Winsor, East Side Prep, Sacred Heart, St. Joseph's, San Francisco Opera, the Boys and Girls Club in San Francisco, and a number of health-related causes. Our focus is on education and children, but we give to a broad array of organizations. It's very rewarding."

Andi and Jeff plan to expand their giving. "There is an amount of money, beyond what we need and will give to our children, that we can give away," she adds. "It's satisfying to make a difference, and I feel good helping to improve the lives of others. I want to involve our sons—sooner rather than later—in our family philanthropy to let them discover the joy in giving."

■ **Gregory C. Carr**. "I care deeply about human rights, the environment, and the arts, and that is where I am going to make a difference," says Greg Carr, discussing his philanthropy. "It's great fun to be passionate about these areas and make something happen."

Carr has a history of making things happen. He co-founded Boston Technology, Inc., in 1986 and eventually became chairman of the global Internet service provider Prodigy, Inc. In 1999, he sold a portion of his interest in Prodigy and formed his own private family foundation. He also made an $18 million gift to the John F. Kennedy School of Government at Harvard to create the Carr Center for Human Rights Policy.

"Human rights is a discipline that needs to be professionalized, and the Carr Center will help bring intellectual rigor to this issue," he says. "I see Harvard assisting human rights organizations around the world with research, teaching, and training on the best practices. I've been able to bring Harvard to my home state of Idaho where the Kennedy School is training local officials on how best to promote human rights."

Carr is also expanding the scope of the natural history museum in Idaho Falls and recently purchased Grendel's Restaurant at 89 Winthrop Street in Cambridge. It will be renovated into a new theater. In addition, he serves on the board of Physicians for Human Rights.

Carr says that managing his foundation is his full-time job. "I enjoy this activity and am using professional skills from my for-profit life to think about what I can achieve philanthropically," he adds. "I spent time thinking about the name of the foundation and decided on a *family* name. The Carr Foundation is for all of my family to work on and be proud of. We are making a statement about what we care about."

Conclusion

Clearly, there are a variety of ways to organize and approach your individual and family philanthropy. The rewards of the effort can be deeply satisfying: making the world a better place and strengthening your family.

In the case of my family, we recently held a meeting of my generation (eight of us, including spouses) to discuss a family gift from my father's donor advised fund. After a debate on the issues of focus and purpose and a subsequent site visit, we settled on one grant to the Kidney Foundation of Massachusetts, since two people in our immediate family have had kidney transplants.

I learned more about my sisters' values as they talked about what was important to them. This was a bonus that I had hoped for, and my family's experience illustrates the continuing value of engaging in family philanthropy.

CHAPTER 8
EPILOGUE

In the long run the possessor of great wealth

is judged in part by the use he makes of his riches,

including in that use his disposal of them at his death.

Charles W. Eliot AB 1853
President of Harvard University, 1869–1909
from *Great Riches* (1906)

I began this book with a series of questions and will end in the same way. What do you and your family *really* value? How can you help to guide your children's life journey? What kind of vision does your family aspire to achieve?

My message is a simple one: The real wealth of your family is not financial. Because of this, your core values and family's vision should be thought through *before* implementing various estate planning strategies. Moreover, you can keep your family's human capital growing over time by thinking periodically about your role and your family's role in promoting the growth and development of family members.

A personal mission statement, an ethical will, or a philosophy of life is a statement to your children of what kind of legacy you want to leave them and how you want to be remembered. Defining a vision for the future is a family exercise others are using. The conversation, the planning, and the journey with your children is what matters most. John O'Neill, a business leadership consultant, says it well in his book *Leadership Aikido*: "A plan is nothing more than a road map to a destination that will leave you changed—a different person from the one that started the trip."

Defining the most important themes surrounding family wealth is something the Rev. Peter J. Gomes thinks about in fresh ways. "My thesis involves the distinction between 'making a living' and 'making a life,'" says Gomes, Plummer Professor of Christian Morals and Pusey Minister in the Memorial Church at Harvard University. "What it means to make a life is difficult to articulate because we are still uneasy talking about money. The problems are: Who gets the money? Do you really know what to do with it? How do you talk about it? There is a conspiracy of silence today, and little serious discourse on the social and moral uses of wealth."

Gomes makes the case for communication concerning our financial wealth and reminds us of the complex place of money in the American landscape, as described by Daphne Merkin in a *New Yorker* article: "Although my family's now-you-see-it, now-you-don't approach to money may have been particularly heated, I slowly came to realize that this private obfuscation was embedded within a larger cultural evasiveness. I noticed that other people were caught in a similarly ambivalent grip. No one was honest about the subject of money; worse yet, not many people seemed to recognize that they were dishonest. People either deified money or demonized it."

Wealth looms large in our society today and is a highly charged part of our lives. It has the power to "create capacity"—to help individuals discover and pursue their calling. But it can also subvert that effort. "Money has profound meaning in our society," says columnist Esther M. Berger in a *Town and Country* article. "It has become a metaphor for many things, some positive (freedom and philanthropy, for example) and some decidedly negative (condescension and control)."

In short, we need to be "awake" to the messages surrounding money that we send to our children and aware of those messages we inherited from our own parents. As Gomes points out, "We need to raise our consciousness about our wealth and the effect of the choices we make."

Thus, the important choices we make about our financial wealth are linked to what we value and are often driven by a strong sense of urgency. These decisions matter on a deeper level because of our own impending death. But the fact that we are going to die can set us free. "The more we refuse to *look* at our own death, the more we repress and deny new possibilities for living," says the Rev. Alan W. Jones, Dean of Grace Cathedral in San Francisco, in his book, *Soul Making*. "We are all going to die, and our life is a movement to that sure end. . . . Meditation on this simple fact has a wonderful way of clearing the mind! It enables us to live every single moment with new appreciation and delight. . . . The willingness to live with the knowledge of our inevitable death enables us to face, more and more, both the freedom and responsibility that life offers. . . . As Don Juan reminds Castaneda: 'In a world where death is a hunter, . . . there is no time for regrets or doubts. There is only time for decisions.'"

Who am I, then, in light of my own mortality? This question leads us to reflect on our legacy—the extension of our life that continues after death. What kind of legacy do we want to leave—to our families, to our society, to the world at large?

Philanthropy has the potential to inspire a personal legacy and allow us to leave a lasting mark. In his book, *The Age of Paradox*, Charles Handy, business consultant and fellow of the London Business School, reflects on the meaning of legacy. Handy writes, "It is a search for a cause. The cause, however, to be truly satisfying must be a 'purpose beyond oneself,' because to be turned in on oneself, said St. Augustine, is the greatest of sins; because we discover ourselves through others, said Jung; because the immortality, for which we all privately long, is really immortality through others."

"Philanthropy is a way for mortals to pursue immortality," concludes Rev. Gomes:

> Wealth is not just private treasure for private use. Money has civic content and society has a claim on our money. The wisdom of "to whom much is given, much is expected" has had a firm place in the moral landscape of the West for thousands of years.
>
> This is not a new mandate, but it is being redefined today. How do I strike a balance between what is good for me and my family, and what is good for society? Building family and building society go together. Money is a means to an end, morally neutral but with public consequences.
>
> How do you want to be remembered? How do you wish history to record you? What lasting imprint do you want to leave on the world? Thinking through what your life is evolving toward is the central task in "making a life." Enjoy what you have by sorting out what to leave. Legacy ought to be a life's work.

Appendix A

FAMILY QUESTIONNAIRE #1
(Harvard University)

1. Which of the following are most important to you? (Please rank them from 1 to 5, with 1 as the highest and 5 as the lowest value.)

   Personal achievement _____   Personal incentive
                                     and hard work _____
   Career success _____
                                     Self-esteem _____
   Financial independence _____
                                     Service to others _____
   Family unity and tradition _____
                                     Permanent legacy _____
   Responsible uses of money _____
                                     Philanthropy _____
   Creativity _____
                                     Volunteerism _____
   Spirituality _____
                                     Other _____
   Community standing _____

2. Who or what were the greatest influences on you in developing your values?

   Parents _____   Mentors _____

   Other relatives _____   Personal experiences _____

   Teachers _____   Other _____

3. How did your family achieve its present financial status?

   Inherited wealth _____   Personal effort _____

   Good fortune _____   Support from others _____

4. Please describe your parents' financial histories.

   _____

   _____

   _____

   _____

5. Which financial values and/or decisions of your parents continue to affect you the most today?

_____

_____

_____

6. How much money do you need to spend each year to live comfortably?

_____

7. Which important values do your children already possess?

_____

_____

_____

How will these values be transmitted to your grandchildren?

_____

_____

_____

8. How wealthy do you want your children (and grandchildren) to become?

_____

_____

_____

Why?

_____

_____

_____

Age	Capital	Income
Twenties	_____	_____
Thirties	_____	_____
Forties	_____	_____

9. What are the pros and cons of leaving substantial wealth to your children?

Benefits _____

Risks _____

10. How much do they know about the inheritance they will receive?

_____

_____

_____

11. How confident are you that your children have the judgment and skills to manage and to use inherited wealth?

_____

_____

_____

12. How philanthropic do you expect your children to be?

_____

Should they be involved in public service?

_____

Do these issues matter to you?

_____

13. Do you feel any personal responsibilities beyond your family?

_____

_____

_____

14. What part does philanthropy play in your own value system?

_____

_____

_____

15. Which institutions have been most important to you in your life?

    _____

    _____

    _____

16. There are three basic beneficiaries of your estate: your heirs, the IRS,
    and the institutions and causes that matter to you.

    What is the current percentage distribution?

    Heirs_____%   IRS_____%   Philanthropy_____%

    What would you like it to be?

    Heirs_____%   IRS_____%   Philanthropy_____%

17. Are you aware of some techniques that can be used to modify these
    percentages to more closely resemble your goals?

    Yes _____

    No _____

FAMILY QUESTIONNAIRE #2
(The Philanthropic Initiative)

1. Considering our history as a family, do we understand and agree on our core family values?

   How would you express them? _____

   _____

   _____

2. Do your values differ from those in your family? If so, how would you express that difference?

   _____

   _____

3. The family is fortunate to have significant resources that can be used to enable its members to further important personal business and philanthropic interests. What is your view of these resources, and what opportunities, risks, and issues do they represent to you?

   _____

   _____

   _____

4. Does a family foundation seem like a good idea? If so, why? If not, why not?

   _____

   _____

   _____

   How do you think a family foundation should be organized?

   _____

   _____

   _____

5. Individually, we have a history of charitable giving and volunteerism. Do we know why we made those gifts of money and time? Do we feel good about our choices? Do we know if our efforts made any difference?

_____

_____

_____

a. Which of our past gifts have given us the most satisfaction?

_____

b. Which have given us the least?

_____

6. As a donor, and perhaps as a trustee of a family foundation, what criteria would you put on proposals before they were funded?

_____

_____

_____

7. Considering the future, what are the things about which you feel passionate? What are the things that really interest you? There are many major issues facing society, including the arts, children's causes, civil rights, education, environment, housing, and abolishing hunger. They are all important, but which ones would you give the highest priority? Which ones do you feel are most important and why?

_____

_____

_____

8. To what extent would you like to be involved in the work of exploring and/or analyzing problems and shaping promising solutions?

_____

_____

_____

9. To develop a process that works for each of us, what steps would be the most helpful for you to learn about the things that interest you?

Research on specific subjects _____

Site visits to nonprofit organizations _____

Background information to read _____

Visits with experts _____

10. How much direct contact with donees would you like to have?

_____

_____

11. Given your other commitments, how much time do you have to devote to philanthropy?

_____

_____

12. Based upon what you know about the family, do you think it is possible to arrive at consensus around giving?

_____

_____

13. Irrespective of consensus, should resources be made available for each individual to give and to use as he or she wishes? If so, what amount could you effectively use in 2001?

_____

_____

14. What level of recognition and visibility interests you?

_____

_____

_____

15. How much risk tolerance do you have? (That is, are these funds to be used as seed capital, or are you more interested in building organizational capacity within existing organizations?)

_____

_____

_____

16. In which geographical range are you most interested in giving help: local, national, global, or some combination of all three?

_____

_____

_____

17. Are you more interested in helping individuals or organizations, or do you wish to affect public policy?

_____

_____

_____

18. Any other ideas or thoughts?

_____

_____

_____

Appendix B

SOME GIFT VEHICLES

There are a number of attractive benefits to creating your own family philanthropic fund. Most important, you are allowed to make income- or estate-tax-deductible gifts to a separate entity while retaining the ability to influence or control—to varying degrees—how the funds are distributed.

There are essentially three kinds of vehicles that individuals can use: the private foundation, the supporting organization, and the donor advised fund. The private foundation permits complete control, the supporting organization allows shared control, and the donor advised fund gives you a significant degree of influence, although there is technically no control.

Private foundations

A private foundation is a trust or corporation created expressly to benefit charitable institutions. The charitable purposes that you support can be broadly or narrowly defined; moreover, you can vary the charitable recipients from year to year.

The private foundation provides the highest degree of personal control of your giving. You alone can decide what institutions to support. You can keep the donated property within your management and control, provide modest employment income to family members, and limit board membership to family members. Most financial advisers agree that $5 million is the minimum amount needed to fund a private foundation indefinitely.

There are a number of disadvantages to using a private foundation. Foremost among these are the limitations on the income tax deductibility of gifts (gifts of appreciated property are deductible only to the extent of your tax cost or basis), minimum distribution requirements, applicability of excise taxes, and various investment restrictions. Additionally, there are administrative costs and reporting requirements.

Supporting organizations

A supporting organization is similar to a private foundation in that it is a freestanding, tax-exempt organization, but it serves to support one or more designated public charities. It is a useful vehicle for donors who want to maintain some investment control or formally involve family members, but who also want to be closely affiliated with one or more specific charitable institutions. The minimum amount necessary to create a supporting organization with Harvard is typically $1 million.

For example, if you want to benefit multiple Harvard Faculties, participate in investment decisions, and involve your children in the philanthropic process, you can create a supporting organization to provide scholarships and fellowships. Each year, the board of the supporting organization meets and designates the investment income for financial aid at different Schools around the University.

Family members may sit on the organization's board, but they must represent less than 50 percent of its directors. For example, the board could consist of the donor, the donor's son or daughter, and three Harvard officers.

Supporting organizations are free of all the rules governing private foundations, avoid the distribution and excise tax requirements, and allow more generous deductibility limitations for charitable gifts. In fact, gifts of appreciated stock are income tax deductible at fair market value.

Donor advised funds

An increasingly popular vehicle among charitably minded individuals who want to be actively involved in the distribution of their gifts but not concerned with the day-to-day investment management is the donor advised fund.

A donor advised fund is a component fund of a public charity or community foundation. It operates somewhat like a private foundation, but it is managed by the public institution and receives more favorable tax treatment. For example, there are no distribution minimums, no excise taxes on investment income, and no cumbersome reporting and administrative requirements. Moreover, the full fair market value of gifts of appreciated stock is tax deductible.

Many public charities and community foundations offer donor advised funds. For example, the Boston Foundation, the New York Community Trust, the United Jewish Appeal, the Fidelity Charitable Gift Fund, and

Harvard University all have plans that allow you to make gifts and then recommend grant distributions to qualified charities anywhere in the United States. Of course, each of these funds has different requirements and minimums. For example, the minimum gift to create a donor advised fund with the New York Community Trust is $10,000, and at Vanguard Charitable Trust it is $25,000, whereas Harvard University requires $250,000, with at least half of the principal dedicated to Harvard.

Many philanthropists have used private foundations, supporting organizations, and donor advised funds to retain a level of control over their charitable dollars and make a significant difference in the lives of the institutions they care about. Today, all three entities continue to be excellent vehicles for saving income and estate taxes and passing on the values of treating wealth responsibly to the next generation.

Appendix C

ADDITIONAL RESOURCES

Organizations

Council on Foundations
1828 L Street NW, Suite 300
Washington, DC 20036
(202) 466-6512 — Fax: (202) 785-3926
http://www.cof.org/

Family Firm Institute
221 North Beacon St.
Boston, MA 02135
(617) 789-4200 — Fax: (617) 789-4220
http://www.ffi.org/

Family Office Exchange
137 North Oak Park Ave., Suite 310
Oak Park, IL 60301
(708) 848-2030 — Fax: (708) 848-2131
http://www.familyoffice.com

Institute for Private Investors
74 Trinity Place
New York, NY 10006
(212) 693-1300 — Fax: (212) 697-2797
http://www.memberlink.net/index.htm

The National Center for Family Philanthropy
1220 Nineteenth St., NW, Suite 804
Washington, DC 20036
(202) 293-3424 — Fax: (202) 293-3395
http://www.ncfp.org

The Philanthropic Initiative, Inc.
77 Franklin St.
Boston, MA 02110
(617) 338-2590 — Fax: (617) 338-2591
http://www.tpi.org

The Inheritance Project
P.O. Box 503
Ivy, VA 22945
(804) 961-0876 — Fax: (804) 244-7880
www.inheritance-project.com

Bibliography

Buford, Bob. *Halftime*. Grand Rapids: Zondervan Publishing House, 1994.

Covey, Stephen R. *The 7 Habits of Highly Effective Families*. New York: Golden Books, 1997.

Dashew, Leslie. *The Best of the Human Side: Managing Our Selves, Our Relationships, and Our Organizations in a Rapidly Changing World*. Tucson: Beowulf Publishing, 1997.

Dreikurs, Rudolph, with Vicki Soltz. *Children: The Challenge*. New York: Hawthorn Books, 1964.

Fritz, Roger. *Wars of Succession: The Blessings, Curses and Lessons That Family-Owned Firms Offer Anyone in Business*. Santa Monica: Merritt Publishing, 1997.

Gersick, Kelin F., John A. Davis, Marion McCollom Hampton, and Ivan Lansberg. *Generation to Generation: Life Cycles of the Family Business*. Boston: Harvard Business School Press, 1997.

Godfrey, Neale S., with Tad Richards. *A Penny Saved: Teaching Your Children the Values and Life Skills They Will Need to Live in the Real World*. New York: Simon & Schuster, 1995.

Grossman, Allen, Christine W. Letts, and William P. Ryan. *High Performance Nonprofit Organizations: Managing Upstream for Greater Impact*. New York: John Wiley & Sons, 1999.

Handy, Charles. *The Age of Paradox*. Boston: Harvard Business School Press, 1994.

Hausner, Lee. *Children of Paradise: Successful Parenting for Prosperous Families*. Los Angeles: Jeremy P. Tarcher, Inc., 1990.

Hughes, James E., Jr. *Family Wealth: Keeping It in the Family*. Princeton Junction, NJ: NetWrx, 1997.

Jaffe, Dennis T. *Working with the Ones You Love: Strategies for a Successful Family Business*. Aspen: Aspen Family Business Group, 1991.

Kinder, George. *The Seven Stages of Money Maturity*. New York: Dell Publishing, 1999.

Lansberg, Ivan. *Succeeding Generations: Realizing the Dream of Families in Business*. Boston: Harvard Business School Press, 1999.

Levinson, Daniel J. *The Seasons of a Man's Life*. New York: Ballantine Books, 1978.

Livingston, Richard and Linda. *Smart & Caring: A Donor's Guide to Major Gifting*. Louisville: RDL Publishing, 1999.

Napier, Augustus Y., with Carl Whitaker, M.D. *The Family Crucible*. New York: Harper & Row, 1978.

Needleman, Jacob. *Money and the Meaning of Life*. New York: Doubleday, 1991.

O'Neil, John. *Leadership Aikido*. New York: Three Rivers Press, 1997.

O'Neil, John R. *The Paradox of Success*. New York: Jeremy P. Tarcher/Putnam, 1993.

Paisner, Marshall B. *Sustaining the Family Business: An Insider's Guide to Managing Across Generations*. Reading, PA: Perseus Books, 1999.

Pearl, Jayne A. *Kids and Money: Giving Them the Savvy to Succeed Financially*. Princeton: Bloomberg Press, 1999.

Pipher, Mary. *The Shelter of Each Other: Rebuilding Our Families*. New York: Ballantine Books, 1996.

Reimer, Jack, and Nathaniel Stampfer. *So That Your Values Live On: Ethical Wills and How to Prepare Them*. Woodstock, NY: Jewish Lights Publishing, 1991.

Rosenberg, Claude, Jr. *Wealthy and Wise*. Boston: Little, Brown, 1994.

Rottenberg, Dan. *The Inheritor's Handbook: A Definitive Guide for Beneficiaries*. Princeton: Bloomberg Press, 1999.

Spence, Linda. *Legacy: A Step-by-Step Guide to Writing Personal History*. Athens, OH: Swallow Press/Ohio University Press, 1997.

Williams, Roy O. *For Love & Money*. Marina, CA: Monterey Pacific Institute, 1997.

Internet Resources

Financial Sites

www.kiplinger.com

Kiplinger.com offers information and advice on almost every aspect of business and finance: investments, retirement, taxes, etc. Users can also access articles from *Kiplinger's Magazine* on the site.

www.quicken.com

On Quicken.com, users can access business news, get information on topics like investing, taxes, and retirement, and track their own individual investment portfolios.

www.armchairmillionaire.com

This site, part of Investorama's network of financial sites, offers investment information and advice as well as chat rooms and message boards on related topics.

http://finance.yahoo.com

This Yahoo! finance site offers stock market information and news, stock quotes, and other related information and articles.

www.schwab.com

The Charles Schwab site includes information about investment and retirement planning, as well as stock market news and quotes. Users can open and access accounts on the site.

www.fool.com

The Motley Fool Web site includes stock quotes and market information, research on specific stocks, and personal finance information.

www.personalwealth.com

This site includes market and investment news, analysis, and advice, as well as information on mutual funds, bonds, and various industries.

www.andrewtobias.com

Andrew Tobias, author of numerous books, has a daily column on his site as well as a mutual fund cost calculator and links to other sites of interest.

www.bobbrinker.com

This site, produced by Bob Brinker, host of the *MoneyTalk* radio show, provides information about *MoneyTalk*, excerpts from the *Marketimer* newsletter, and educational information on topics such as mutual funds and retirement planning.

www.moolera.com

This site provides information for investment beginners, including the following topics: retirement planning, mutual funds, stocks, and basics of investing.

www.mycfo.com

This site provides financial services, including estate planning and coordinating charitable activities, to high-net-worth individuals.

www.vanguard.com

Vanguard's site features stock market and fund highlights, information and guidance on a host of topics from taxes to financial planning, and an opportunity to open and access accounts.

www.gomez.com

Produced by Gomez Advisors, this site offers comparative information about online businesses, ranging from personal finance to health information.

www.businessfamilies.com

Business Families Foundation is a nonprofit organization dedicated to the needs and concerns of families who own and manage private companies. They offer educational programs designed to assist with issues facing business families.

www.talkcity.com

Essentially a "chat site," this site allows individuals to enter chat rooms to discuss issues related to business, finance, and real estate.

www.wfn.com

Women's Financial Network, Inc. is a comprehensive financial site designed for women, where users can find financial advisers, access bank and brokerage accounts, track and research investments, and obtain other types of financial information.

www.estateplanninglinks.com

This site provides links to resources for estate planning and related areas.

www.independentmeans.com

This site provides financial information, products, and services for teenage girls and their mentors. Independent Means offers one-day conferences, summer camps, and a national business plan competition.

For Kids and Parents

www.kidsbank.com

Produced by Sovereign Bank, this site explains the basics of banking and money through guided stories and games.

www.ncfe.org

The National Center for Financial Education Web site has an online catalog of children's books about money as well as information on teaching children about money.

www.littlejason.com/lemonade

Lemonade Stand is a game that teaches children about supply and demand in business.

www.connectforkids.com

Connect for Kids serves as a resource for adults on a variety of issues and topics concerning children. Features include a weekly newsletter, articles, and volunteer and organization information.

Online Donation Sites

The following sites allow individuals to search for nonprofit organizations in a number of different categories, find detailed information about each group, and make donations online.

www.giveforchange.com
www.charitable-way.com
www.givenation.com
www.allcharities.com
www.myfoundation.org

Philanthropy

www.philanthropy.com

The *Chronicle of Philanthropy*'s Web site includes articles from the publication on topics ranging from fundraising to managing nonprofit groups, job openings in the field, and conference and workshop information. Much of the site is restricted to subscribers only.

www.guidestar.org

Guidestar, produced by Philanthropic Research, Inc., is a database of over 620,000 nonprofit organizations in the United States where individuals can search for a particular organization and find a complete report of the charity, including financial information. The site also features current news articles dealing with philanthropy issues.

www.pj.org

Philanthropy News Network Online updates news daily on many topics, such as the following: corporate giving, education, foundations, law, taxes, fundraising, and general giving.

www.philanthropyroundtable.org

This site includes articles from the publication *Philanthropy*, as well as information on upcoming meetings and seminars of the Philanthropy Roundtable, a national association of individual donors, corporations, and foundations.

www.tpi.org

The Philanthropic Initiative, Inc. is a not-for-profit organization that provides research, education programs, and consulting services to individuals, family foundations, and corporations regarding strategic philanthropy planning. The site offers access to publications and research as well as educational programming.

www.women-philanthropy.org

The Women's Philanthropy Institute (WPI) is a nonprofit organization committed to the education and advancement of women as major donors and leaders in the area of philanthropy. The site provides information about upcoming programming and allows individuals to subscribe to their newsletter online.

www.ncfp.org

The National Center for Family Philanthropy, a nonprofit organization, encourages individuals and families to create a philanthropic mission and offers resources to help them in their philanthropic efforts. The site offers access to upcoming workshops, publications, and other resource information.

www.philanthropysearch.com

This site is a search engine for the nonprofit sector. Users can search by category or by key words.

www.plannedgivingtoday.com

The Planned Giving Today site serves as a resource for gift planning professionals. Users can view excerpts from the newsletter and subscribe online.

www.charitablegift.org

Produced by Fidelity Investments, this site showcases their two charitable giving tools: a donor advised fund and a pooled income fund. Users can learn about these tools and open and access accounts.

www.schwabcharitable.org

The Schwab Fund for Charitable Giving site provides users with information about charitable gift accounts, the chance to open and view accounts, and the ability to search for charities through GuideStar.

www.greatergood.com

Consumers can shop online for retail goods with 5 to 15 percent of each purchase going to the charitable organization of their choice.

Philanthropy Resources

www.cof.org

The Council on Foundations, a membership association of foundations and corporations, offers information and resources about and for foundations. The site also contains information about conferences and workshops, job opportunities, and a publications catalog.

www.fdncenter.org

The Foundation Center, a nonprofit organization, provides information on foundations, corporate giving, and related subjects. The site also has an online library to assist users in finding the resources they need.

www.virtualfoundation.org

The Virtual Foundation is an online organization that supports small projects involving the environment, development, and health. The proposals are posted on the site where individuals and groups can review them and make donations.

Volunteer Sites

www.helping.org

Helping.org, created by the AOL Foundation, is an online resource designed to assist individuals in finding volunteer and donation opportunities as well as assisting charitable organizations in implementing the use of the Internet in their planning.

www.volunteermatch.org

Produced by ImpactOnline, VolunteerMatch provides individuals with a way to search for volunteer opportunities online. Charitable organizations are able to post their volunteer needs on the site.

www.idealist.org

On this site, users can search for nonprofit organizations, access job and internship listings, and find volunteer opportunities.

www.mentoring.org

The National Mentoring Partnership serves as a resource for mentors and mentoring groups across the country. From this site, users can search for and learn more about existing opportunities in their communities.

Career Sites

www.vault.com

This site provides detailed information about many industries, including news, career advice and guides, message and job boards, and prolific research on companies in each industry.

www.wetfeet.com

This site offers users the opportunity to research careers, individual companies, and more than 30 industries.

CHARLES W. COLLIER

Charles W. Collier is the senior philanthropic adviser at Harvard University. He has also served Phillips Academy, Andover; Dartmouth College; Brown University; and Princeton University. A nationally recognized expert on planned giving and family philanthropy, Collier has been a speaker at many conferences, including the National Committee on Planned Giving, the Council for the Advancement and Support of Education, and the National Association of Independent Schools. He has written widely on the subjects of family wealth and charitable giving and has been published in *Trusts & Estates*, *Advancing Philanthropy,* and *Planned Giving Today*. Collier serves on advisory committees of the National Center for Family Philanthropy and The Philanthropic Initiative, Inc. Over the past twenty-five years he has worked with hundreds of individuals and families to help them think through the questions addressed in this book. He graduated from Phillips Academy, Andover, and holds an AB from Dartmouth College and an MTS from Harvard Divinity School. He and his wife and two sons live in Wellesley, Massachusetts and Dublin, New Hampshire.